THE CHI
CODE

—

By Thomas Dockstader

Printed in the United States of America

Publisher's Cataloging-in-Publication data

Dockstader, Thomas

The Chi Code / Thomas Dockstader

ISBN 978-0-578-67457-5

First Edition

14 13 12 11 10 / 10 9 8 7 6 5 4 3 2 1

DEDICATION

This book is dedicated to all of the people who
are walking through the fires of life and those
who have made it to the other side.

TABLE OF CONTENTS

Part II - CONDITIONING   45

FOREWORD

"Truth does not conflict with truth... indeed all truth
may be circumscribed into one great whole"
- D. Todd Christofferson

Thomas and I met through a modern-day matchmaker. My sister had recommended the service after I had literally tried everything else to find "Mr. Right" to no avail. In today's high-speed digital world using a matchmaker may seem like a very old-school way to meet someone, but after years of dismal failures in the dating world my faith in finding someone was fading and I was open to meeting someone in an unconventional way. In retrospect, knowing the different directions our lives were heading in, it would have been nearly impossible for Thomas and I to meet in any other way.

The first thing I noticed about Thomas were his looks, after all it was a first date. He was tall, dark and handsome, about 6' 2" and incredibly well built. I was pleasantly surprised by his down-to-earth personality and amazed to find he didn't have the oversized ego that typically comes with men of his stature. The conversation was so good on our first date that we stayed at the restaurant for hours talking after we had finished our meal. Thomas was extremely honest—another rare find on a date—and his openness drew me in. Before the date, the matchmaker had instructed me "not to talk too much" to keep him interested and motivated to ask me out on a second date, which was ironic because the men always seemed to do most of the talking on these dates. She had also sent me (and not him) an email advising me not to talk about "money, sex, or politics" at dinner. Thomas and I ended up talking about all three taboo subjects and a dozen other controversial topics I usually steered clear of on first dates. He was so fun to talk with; I literally wanted to hear his insights on everything. Despite the matchmaker's trepidation, Thomas did ask me out on a second date where the conversation was even better than our first date. I didn't realize it at the time, but I had met the man I was going to marry. He truly was the "one" in 7.8 billion people I'd been searching for.

At first glance, based on the in-depth profiles of us the matchmaker had prepared, Thomas and I seemed like an unlikely match. Education is very important to me. I graduated top of my class, went on to get a master's degree at the University of Oxford in England and earned a Ph.D. in Strategy and Entrepreneurship. I have years of experience working for some of the most innovative companies in the world as a consultant in Silicon Valley and now work as a professor at a university. I'm well read, having studied under some of the brightest and most prestigious scholars in the world. In contrast, Thomas dropped out of school at the age of 14 to start working. Although we didn't have much in common in the way of education, Thomas and I both grew up in religious families. However, I am a devout member of my faith and it plays an integral role in my life. While Thomas was highly opposed to organized religion as a result of his upbringing and considered himself spiritual, but not religious. In addition, we had very different tastes in movies and literature and a million other things that would make us an unlikely match. However, we quickly realized that when you looked beyond these superficial differences we were both very similar at the core. This commonality served as our primary bond in the beginning and has become the foundation we have built a lasting relationship on. While we were dating, our conversations would often involve Thomas discussing his insights about life and me sharing with him countless books, research, and scholarly articles from around the world that taught the same principles. We quickly came to realize that despite our very different approaches and backgrounds, we were both seeking and fascinated with the same truths.

The Chi Code is one of those truths. It is different from the countless self-help books out there because it doesn't just tell you, it actually shows you, how to make the changes you want in your life. Like all great truths, Chi Code principles are simple; it is the consistent action of putting them into practice that gives them a profound effect.   Thomas truly lives the principles he teaches in The Chi Code. Moreover, instead of being hesitant to share how he changed his life, Thomas is completely forthcoming about the process and sincerely aims to help anyone seeking to "recode" their own lives.

Thomas's approach is unique because he doesn't try to hide the negative parts of his past and only highlight his positive accomplishments. He realizes that it is the combination of the positive and the negative together that make him the man he is today. This is what the Chinese refer to as your "chi". According to Chinese philosophy, chi is a vital force thought to be inherent in all things. The unimpeded circulation of chi and a balance of its negative and positive forms in the body are held to be essential to good health in traditional Chinese medicine.

Deep down, when we reflect on our lives, we all have a code we live by. A set of values adapted from our upbringing, a mantra about the way life should be, or a belief that there is some higher purpose to our lives. Each of us has a philosophy explaining or driving why we do what we do. Do you know what yours is? When Thomas first shared this idea with me, I denied it. He challenged me to look back to my

childhood for answers I had been searching for. I told him I didn't believe that and refused to do it. He lovingly persuaded me to humor him by doing one simple exercise. I told him of an early memory in elementary school. As Thomas walked me through it, for the first time I could see how I was still carrying that childhood experience with me in my professional and personal life as an adult. I was shocked. I had never made the connection before. Thomas and I are married now and expecting our first child. We talk about our coding more than ever as we continually seek to improve our own lives and influence, for good, the code of our children.

The Chi Code teaches true principles that when applied to your life can help you achieve the balance and enlightenment you've been searching for. I hope when you read this book the concepts and ideas will resonate as true for you as they did for me. Instead of thinking you need a lot more money, time, or resources to obtain the results you've always wanted, hopefully you'll realize that the change you're seeking is already within your grasp. As you read this book, you'll learn to find your chi by accepting both the positive and negative in your life. Then the book will teach you step by step how to start writing or re-writing the code of the life you've always envisioned for yourself. I hope you find what you've been looking for, I did.

Heidi Noelle Herrick Dockstader, PhD

HOW TO USE THIS BOOK

Consult not your fears but your hopes and your dreams.
Think not about your frustrations, but about your
unfulfilled potential. Concern yourself not with what you tried
and failed in, but with what it is still possible for you to do.
-Pope John XXIII

We're all coded with our past experiences. Sometimes that coding leads us in the right direction, but often it leads us in the wrong direction. How your life's experience, or your Chi Code, affects you is an individual thing. The concept of "Chi" comes from Chinese philosophy and means "life force". It is the life-giving, vital energy that unites body, mind and spirit and animates the body internally.

This book is part memoir and part self-help book. It's here to guide you through your own journey by allowing you to see how I've healed through mine. Make sure to start at the prologue, this is an important start of the story. For you to get something out of it, you have to exert some effort. Don't just sit back and read it, put these principles into practice in your life.

At the end of every chapter, you'll find questions that will help you relate what you've just read to what you're personally experiencing. Write down your answers to the questions, even though I know it's easy to just gloss over them. These moments of reflection on your own reality will be valuable and will empower you to make the changes to your code necessary to realize your goals and create the life you envision for yourself.

Your life is completely unique from mine, but we're the same in that we all have baggage from our past that we must deal with in the present if we want to create a different future. Reading this book, and more importantly relating it to yourself, is a positive step in the direction of bringing your past into the present. The hard truth is that you're carrying it with you either way. How you carry your experiences with you is a determining factor in whether you will live a broken and painful existence or a happy and fulfilled life.

You deserve to be happy. You deserve to feel whole. You deserve to unlock your Chi Code and create the life that you've dreamed of.

PROLOGUE
ROCK BOTTOM

But in the end, one needs more courage to live than to kill himself.
-Albert Camwus

"I'm done with this life. I just don't want it anymore."

For the last three days I've found the bottom of glass after glass of cold, clear vodka. The island in the kitchen is crowded with empty bottles. They have a fuzzy reflection in the dark countertop, creating the illusion that there are even more of them. For years, this has been a regular pattern for me. I stay wet with alcohol during the week, but on the weekends I drench myself in it. Vodka is now my closest relationship, a quiet friend who is always there for me.

Alcohol dulls my senses and opens up my mind. The more I drink, the more rambling my thoughts get. Things seem somehow clearer, yet more confusing at the same time. I don't remember the way I am without drinking. I don't know if there is even a "me" without drinking. Either way, I don't want to remember it. I just want all of it to be over. Everything. No more guilt, no more burdens, no more failures. I keep looking back on my life and all I can see is mistake after mistake after mistake. Any bright spots that might have been there have been erased, colored over in black by my sins.

This deep into the drinking I am at war with myself. I've felt this way so long that I don't even realize how wrong it is. One side of me is pushing me forward, to go ahead and do it. The other is yanking me away from the gun.

Just do it Thomas. You're a burden on everyone in your life. Your son deserves better than you. Your family deserves better than you. You know you're going to hell anyway so why are you waiting? Tonight is the night. Don't be a wimp. Just go get the gun.

You'll be a bigger burden if you kill yourself. You saw what your dad's death did to your mom. Yours will break her. No one else gets to escape their problems and you damn well don't deserve to. You deserve to stay on this earth and suffer. Escape with that gun is too easy for you.

This back and forth has been going on in my head for days now, driving me to the point of insanity. I get another glass and pour another shot, then sit down in the recliner to see if the war inside of my head will take a break. On a normal night, the second voice would be louder. It would keep me in reality and less likely to actually do anything. The logical side of me is fully aware of how devastating it would be to my family if I shot myself. We drifted apart after my dad died from cancer, falling down into a pit of sadness that I didn't think we'd ever climb out of. His death was ten years ago and we're all still reeling from it. A suicide would be worse. I know that, when I'm more sober than I am now.

The gun is upstairs in my bedroom. It's secure in a lockbox requiring a code to open it. I have intentionally put a series of roadblocks in my way. In the religion I grew up in., we weren't allowed to have guns, even though they were legal and easy to get in Utah. I didn't grow up around guns or shoot them with my dad.

It had been more than ten years since I'd left my strict faith. In that time I'd abandoned many tenants of my former faith, but I was still cautious about having a gun in the house, especially now that I had a young son who spent half of his time with me. I knew that the most likely outcome with a firearm in the home would be for him or me to get hurt. So when I bought the gun I put it in a safe place. My son has always been the world to me. I never let my alcoholism endanger him. Even if I didn't see a future for myself, I wanted my son to have one.

The gun is in a lockbox for a reason Thomas. Just leave it there. Drink yourself into darkness and go to sleep.

A few weeks earlier I'd decided to buy a gun. In my mind I thought it would be terrible to have the courage and the will to kill myself, but not have the means. Sparing no expense, I bought a thousand dollar .45 with hollow point bullets. There would be no question that if I did decide to take my own life, this weapon would do the job. Completely. No worrying about surviving with half a face or barely hanging on dependent on life-support. This gun was big and bad enough to bring me death, if death was what I decided I wanted. That's the feeling of control that I craved, even though it terrified me. The terror motivated me to put a series of safeguards in place. I bought a lock-box with a code, secured the gun and put it in my bedroom closet. I forced myself to have to think it through. I knew that I was in a dark place and that it was a bad idea for me to have the temptation right there in front of me.

Most of the time I was aware that I was in a dangerous place. But on this hot summer night in Salt Lake City after midnight with a skin full of clear vodka, the part of me that wanted to die was glad that I could go upstairs and get the gun. The desire grew with every passing minute.

Walking up the stairs, I hold onto the rail even though I don't need to steady myself. Almost anyone else would be face planting into the stairs if they had the same quantities of alcohol in them, but not me. One reason that I drank so heavily is that I had a high tolerance for it. I hold onto the rail not because I'm drunk, but because I'm afraid of what's about to happen and I can't stop myself.

The gun is right there in your closet. Just keep on going up those stairs to get it. The faster you get this done, the faster everyone can move on without you. When it's all over, no one will remember you anyway and that's better for them. You know it is.

Picking up the .45 out of the box, I hold it in my right hand. The metal and wood are smooth and cold on my palm. When my fingers wrap around it, I feel a rightness that I haven't been able to find at the bottom of hundreds of bottles of vodka. Somehow the fire of the alcohol and the fire of the gun seem like they go together. This is the night. This is the place. It's almost like I've stepped out of my body, out of the void that's swallowed me up for the last few years. The world makes a scary kind of sense again with the weight of the gun in my hand. My salvation seems to be right here in the barrel of this handgun. I'm terrified of it, but I'm determined to use it.

There's just a faint light from the streetlamps streaming in through the front windows and the gun in my hand looks out of place against my jeans and tennis shoes. I walk back down the stairs to the living room, gun in hand. The feeling's not that different from the drugs I've abused, the way the power of the thing pulls you into another place. I'm on an edge, totally unable to see anything ahead of me but an endless sea of darkness and despair.

There's only one way to end the pain. You're going to hell anyway, and you know you don't care. Hell would be a better place than this. You're a damn drunk bastard, so even if hell is worse, then it's what you deserve.

There's a numbness that accompanies the kind of deep depression I'm experiencing. Some of it can be attributed to the alcohol, but really the alcohol is masking a deeper numbness. It's dulling my mind, making me feel pressure to get it over with. I'm feeling oddly driven. My whole life I felt like things outside of my control were batting me around. Like my 10 siblings batted me around growing up. Like my religion emotionally batted me around for every sin I committed. I hated feeling like I didn't have control over anything in my life. Now I had control in the shape of this .45. I wanted control, it was what I'd been looking for but the fear of pulling the trigger was countering that high. It's frustrating because what I want is for it to be easy and to feel good.

It's not going to be easy, Thomas. It's going to be horrible and you're going to leave everyone in worse shape than they are in already. Put the gun down on the table and go to bed.

My eyes trace the edges of the pistol. The gun is heavy and huge. The metal doesn't feel as cool anymore now that I've been holding it for a few minutes. The gun is the same temperature as my hand and almost feels like it's a part of me. I'm starting to feel that I'm ready to do it. One bang, and then a release. I imagine how peaceful death will be. When I think about the end of my life, it's the calmness that I can't wait to feel. If I can swallow my fear then it'll be over in a matter of seconds. I want to feel peace, more than I've wanted anything in many years. It feels good to actually want something again, but strange to want something so gruesome. I don't even care what's on the other side heaven or hell. I just want it over. Hell is fine with me, I deserve it.

Looking around my living room, I say a silent goodbye to the world and lift the gun up towards my mouth. Then I notice the couch. Then the rug. Then the television.

If you blow your brains out right here, you're going to make a mess. Someone is going to have to come in here and clean you off the walls. They'll have to throw out your couch and wipe you from the windows. Your mom is going to be washing curtains and scrubbing you off the floor on her hands and knees. Can you even kill yourself right? Thomas you really are a worthless piece of shit.

I can't do it here. I've felt like a burden to everyone my entire life. I'm determined not to be a burden to someone in death, if I can help it.

Even under the haze of the alcohol I try to think logically. My blinds are open and I can clearly see the front lawn, on the corner is a patch of green grass. It's perfect. I live alone, and if I shoot myself in my living room not only will it create a mess, but I probably won't be found for a while. My family went through so much when my dad died in a hospital. I don't want to further traumatize my mom or one of my brothers when they find my body decomposing in days or a week. I need to be decisive and get the job done, but I also want to have a neat and orderly end. In the corner of my yard a passerby will see me lying there and call the authorities. It will likely be someone who doesn't know me well and won't be as impacted seeing the dead body of a stranger.

Yes, this is definitely the solution. I'll go outside and blow my brains out on the front lawn. Less mess for someone to clean up and I can die knowing that I've caused the least amount of trouble for the people I leave behind. Gun in hand, thinking I've solved the problem I walk out the front door and down to the lawn. The sky is deep and dark despite the fuzzy lights of Salt Lake City all around me. I'm surrounded by thousands of people, yet I'm completely alone. I can do this, I tell myself, I can get the release that I so desperately need.

I'm standing my face turned up to the sky breathing in air for the last time. There's a gentle summer breeze and it catches the edges of my sleeves. The wind feels nice on my face. I'm terrified but coming to peace with my decision; I know I can do this.

Just do it already, Thomas. Put the gun in your mouth and get it over with. You're stalling again. Don't be a wimp.

I lift the gun, my right hand drawing the barrel closer to my head. My finger is on the trigger.

What are you doing? This thing might not even fire. What if it doesn't go off? How have you not thought to check? You're going to screw this up like you screw up everything.

I turn the gun away from my head, point it high over the wall away from my house and fire two rounds. The sound echoes through the neighborhood, louder than I expected. The gun is in good working order. I know it'll do the job if I can just muster the courage to pull the trigger. The violence of the gun going off shakes me a little, makes my mind wonder how the force is going to feel when it's directed inside my body. Suddenly I'm afraid of the pain and the finality of my decision. I'm not an indecisive person, not even when I'm wasted, but the conflict within me is paralyzing. The journey towards this moment over the last weeks and months has been building like a boat in a storm impossible to navigate. I am lost in a sea of self-loathing and fear.

While lowering the gun, I look around to see if the shots I fired have awoken any neighbors. I don't want to disturb anyone, sympathetic to the parents who will need to go to work in a few hours so they can feed their kids and pay their mortgages. The street is completely quiet. The concept of time becomes hazy when I'm this wasted. I don't really know what time it is, hell I can barely tell what day it is. The stillness suggests it's deep into the night, after midnight but well before five a.m. I have only slept a few odd hours in the past three days.

What about your son? Have you even thought about him you selfish bastard? No one knows your financial situation or how to get into your bank account. You should at least leave him the money and the house. You're going to kill yourself and leave him with so many unanswered questions.

I've been on my own since I was 15 and no one knows how to access anything that I've acquired, which presents another mess for them to clean up. I've not left a note or instructions, I've just been thinking about myself again.

That's all you ever do is think about yourself you damn drunk. You're drinking away all your money and everyone knows it. They all know you're a failure because you are a failure. You know it. When you're gone they'll all have easier lives.

These negative feelings are frustrating and confusing, I want to be done with them and my life.

You're not ever going to stop drinking. Your addiction's too bad, you're too far gone to be saved. There's something wrong with you. You're coded wrong and you know it. No one will ever be able to fix you.

I squint my eyes and try to refocus my mind. The gun is at my side, my finger still wrapped around the trigger. I'm shaking it back and forth just a little, feeling the weight of it in my hand. I'm committed to killing myself now, but I'm worried that I'm going to do it the wrong way. From childhood I've carried burdens of guilt and they are echoing inside of my head now. Every sin I've ever committed and every vice I've been taught would send me to the center of a burning hell when this life is over. It's too much for me to bare anymore.

Your mom is going to be so mad at you. She'll remember the last time she talked to you and she'll blame herself for your stupidity. You're going to get your release and leave her here with nothing but pain.

My cell phone is in my pocket. I switch the gun to my left hand and pull my phone out with my right hand. I swipe up and press my mom's name. "Mom, I love you. You've been a wonderful mom to me, even when I've been terrible. Thank you for everything." Next to her name is my youngest sister's name. Mary has been a support to me in my darkest times over the last few years. "Mary, you're a great sister and I've been lucky to have you. I love you little sis." Sending out these messages to my mom and my sister makes me feel more at peace with what I feel I need to do. It doesn't seem like I'm screwing up my family's lives as much as it did before. Maybe now I can do this and they can move on.

You're stalling again Thomas. You deserve to end it because they don't deserve to have to carry you anymore. You've said your goodbyes and now it can just be over.

Slipping my phone back into my pocket, I shift the gun back to my right hand. It molds right back into my grasp. All around me is darkness.

PART I - DECODING

WHEN YOU GIVE UP IT MEANS YOU NEVER WANTED IT.

—KENDRICK LAMAR

CHAPTER 1
TRUE SELF PORTRAIT

The things which hurt instruct.
- Benjamin Franklin

The darkness didn't last. It never does, no matter how much we believe it's going to.

I woke up on the couch the next morning, empty and disoriented, with three pairs of eyes staring at me. My head felt as empty as my soul had the night before. My mom, sister, and brother stood over me looking down, each face a mixture of accusation and concern.

In the middle of the night I'd sent texts to members of my family to tell them that I loved them. Even though I wanted to kill myself, I had this backward notion that if I did it the "right" way I would bare less guilt and my family would hurt less. The point of killing myself was not to punish anyone and I never wanted to cause the people I loved to feel sadness. In my alcohol-impaired and depressed mental state, the only solution I could see was to end my life. Suicide is an inherently selfish act, but feeling suicidal is not an emotion to be ashamed of. Standing in my front yard with a gun in one hand and my phone in the other, it never occurred to me what my family would do when they received those texts. I somehow thought the messages would be a comfort. Later my family explained to me that receiving my good-bye texts in the middle of the night woke them up to how bad my mental state had deteriorated.

Up to this point in my life, I'd never attempted anything like suicide. I'd done stupid things, but nothing that would land me in jail or that I thought would hurt the people I loved. I'd gone so far down the rabbit hole that I couldn't see how far from reality I'd strayed and I didn't know how to stop or climb back out into the daylight.

I wasn't the only one in my family who'd struggled with addiction, not by a long shot. When I wasn't drinking, I'd stepped in to help my brothers and sisters, given them support and taken them to task for their mistakes. I held fast to the false idea that of all my siblings I was the one who had it together. In my mind, I was a careful and controlled alcoholic. My family members were all aware of my alcohol problem, but in my hypocritical spiral out of control, lying to myself about my own self-portrait was essential. I lied to myself about who was at fault for the problems in my life and what had to be done to change the parts of my life I was dissatisfied with. I lied to myself about a lot of stuff for a long time.

There had been moments of clarity in my life before this point, many of them. You know who you are, you can't escape your true self-portrait. What we do is to paint over that truth, again and again, layer after layer, because we falsely believe it's easier to hide the cracks with a fresh coat of paint than to take on the work of a complete remodel of ourselves. Underneath all of those layers is the reality of who you are. Whatever is under all those layers of self-denial, your true self-portrait is not bad. We are all the results of coding, years of experiences from birth until now that have shaped and molded us into the people we've become. The problem is that until you do the work to find out your coding, you will keep trying to cover up what you think is terrible. I'm here to tell you that who you are under your layers isn't terrible. You might believe that you're broken or damaged. You might think that whatever struggles you've been through in life has made you less than other people. These are lies. We all tell ourselves lots of lies. When I stopped lying to myself the morning after my attempted suicide, my life started changing for the better.

JOLTING AWAKE

The gun changed everything for me that day. Later, after my head cleared, I remembered more of what had happened the previous night. I had put the cold, wide gun barrel in my mouth, my index finger on the trigger. One more second and it would have been over. I started to pull, then everything that I'd leave undone flashed through my mind and I made the quick decision it would be better to wait until I'd settled my affairs, then I'd kill myself. I reasoned with myself that I wanted to do it right, after all, you only get one chance to kill yourself. I took my finger off the trigger, lowered the gun and walked up my front stairs back into the house. Exhausted from the internal war with myself I laid the gun on the table and passed out cold on the couch.

This was rock bottom for me. Everyone has their own rock bottom; for some people it's much lower down than for others. I don't know that you have to hit rock bottom before you can affect real change, but for me it was necessary. Harry Potter author J.K. Rowling once said "Rock bottom became the foundation on which I rebuilt my life." For me it wasn't just hitting rock bottom, I had to make sense of what rock bottom meant to me. There's no magic that's going to rescue you when you go off a cliff in your life. If you don't use the crash to wake yourself up, it doesn't mean a damn thing. No one is coming to save you, you have to save yourself.

My family came to my house that morning wanting to help me. They loved me and wanted to make things better by pulling me out of my dark hole. Unfortunately, they couldn't. My mom showed her deep concern. We'd lost my dad years before and she knew how difficult it is to bury a loved one. The worst thing I can imagine is losing a child, and here was my mother staring into the face of a child she loved confronted with that terrible possibility. She comforted me, her hand on my back, her voice low and calm but also stern saying this could not happen again, my sister seemed at a loss, unsure of what to do next. She talked about ways I could get support and things I needed to change in my life. She realized I needed help, but had no idea where to start. My brother was just angry with me. His low tolerance for other people's mistakes and desire to protect my mom and sisters from the harm I had almost inflicted on them manifested in fury. We ended up yelling at each other until he marched out of my house, slamming the door behind him.

When my family left that morning, they took my gun with them.

LYING TO MYSELF

Over the years of my life up to that point, I'd built up this crystal clear view of myself. I knew who I was, I had supreme confidence in it.

- I was successful.

- I was hardworking.

- I had plenty of money in the bank.

- I was good to my family.

- I was good to my friends.

- I was a good father.

- I had bad taste in the people that I surrounded myself with, attracting friends and relationships that treated me poorly and took advantage of my generosity.

None of the things I had told myself were true. None of it. I'd created a whole life built on lying to myself about who I really was. The drinking fed into the lying, a way to numb myself and push down the pain and hypocrisy.

- I wasn't successful. I was barely getting by in every job I had worked, walking in hungover every morning from the previous night's drinking and fighting with my coworkers and bosses.

- I wasn't hardworking, I put in the minimal amount of work I could to maintain my image.

- I did have money in the bank, but I was nowhere near my potential.

- I kept my family at arms-length and expected them to enable my bad behavior.

- I used my friendships to prop up my false sense of success.

- I did the essentials with my son, taking care of his needs but not putting in the emotional work of nurturing that every child deserves.

- I didn't choose bad people as friends and romantic partners; I was the bad person in these relationships blaming my failings on others instead of taking personal responsibility for my character flaws.

It's all spin when you're spinning out of control. The hardest thing to do is to look back and acknowledge that you've let yourself and the people you care about down. I get it. I've been there. What must happen is an honest personal inventory and acceptance of the truth that you cannot move forward if you're lying to yourself. That doesn't mean you have to tell other people everything, but you do have to tell yourself the truth about what's really going on.

A great deal of what I've found to be helpful is mirrored in the twelve-step program. Honestly, it's mirrored in a lot of programs out there because the path to personal empowerment and freedom is always going to flow along a similar path. The constant in all of these programs is that *you* are making *your* life better. You have to fix it. You have to do something, you can't keep lying to yourself and expect your life to improve.

I disagree with self-help programs that focus on making amends with others early in the process. It's not going to fix you. I believe you have to start by making restitution with yourself. In my experience, once you've worked on you, made your own life functional and are moving forward, then making amends with others will happen naturally. The reparations will be long-lasting, unforced, and genuine. Anyone who has struggled with going down the wrong path in life due to addiction or other self-destructive behaviors, will have hurt people they care about. Remember the person you hurt first and the most often is yourself, so start with you.

ACCOUNTABILITY

I went through my life blaming my problems on everyone else. Why did my parents raise me a certain way? Why did my brothers hurt me when we were growing up? Why did women betray me? Why did my bosses treat me unfairly?

No one else was, or is, the problem in my life. I am the only problem I have to solve. No one else is the problem in your life. You are the only person who can solve your problems. Personal accountability is a willingness to explain one's actions and to admit being the cause of a problem. It's the toughest paradigm shift you're ever going to face, but it's also the most transformative change you'll ever make in your life. When you stop being afraid of accountability, on the other side you'll find empowerment.

It's all about you. Once you take responsibility for what's going on in your life, you stop feeling out of control and you start making changes to yourself. Your actions start speaking for you, so you don't need to go around making amends to everyone in your life. Words are just words, actions speak louder. Taking accountability and making real change in your life is what everyone wants you to do, they don't want to hear you just talk about changing your life. How many people do you know who have talked about changing, but never do? They announce how they're going to stop cheating or lying or drinking, but later you find out that it was just lip service, they're still doing the same bad behaviors. Don't talk about stopping the negative things you're doing, just stop doing them.

Saying you're sorry without action is just manipulation. We are all guilty of it, every single one of us. Apologizing becomes a reflex, it's a way to mitigate the backlash and protect yourself from the full consequences of the horrible things you're doing. To sincerely change you must own those aspects of yourself that you fear. You must face them head-on instead of hiding behind "I'm sorry." This is the first step you MUST take, if you are going to transform your life. Resolve never to apologize again unless you have an action plan to prevent the same thing from happening in the future. Even with small things. To affect real and lasting change in your life, you must end the dangerous and destructive defense mechanism of apologizing. It's a hard habit to break, but it's an important first step to turning your life around.

After my suicide attempt, I kicked myself into high gear making numerous personal changes. I had started on similar paths and failed several times before, but this time things were fundamentally different because I was accountable to myself for my successes and failures.

There is no such thing as an overnight fix. You can hit that rock bottom and still not change. I failed a lot at first. Over time, I've found that I fail less often, but I'm still improving on many aspects of my life every single day. The difference is now I'm taking personal responsibility for my failings--and my successes.

Blaming other people for your problems is living a lie. Blaming your coding for your current actions is living a lie. You can use your past to unlock your future, but that doesn't free you from being accountable for the things that you did on the way to where you are or the negative things you're doing now.

What did happen the night I almost ended my life is I quit cold turkey blaming other people for my problems. It was no longer my boss's fault or my girlfriend's fault or my family's fault. My actions were my fault. If I messed up and took a drink, well that was on me. If I got angry and yelled at someone, I was responsible for the outburst. If I didn't fulfill my dreams, I had no one to blame but myself.

You can eliminate the triggers for the behaviors that you don't want in your life anymore, not by transforming your environment or controlling other people, but by transforming and controlling yourself. So often we want to blame other people for our problems because we incorrectly assume we will feel better if the responsibility is on someone else. I fall into that trap, we all do. What I didn't realize was that I was also giving away my personal power. When you put the responsibility for your life on other people you also give away the power to effect real change in your life. Your failures are someone else's responsibility, but so is the credit for your successes, neither lie is true. When you tell yourself "Oh woe is me", you have no path to fix it. You can't control other people. You can only control yourself. The man I was when I sat around blaming everyone else for my problems is a completely different person than the man I am today. That person is a stranger I wouldn't recognize now.

CHANGING YOUR CODE—CHAPTER 1

What is a moment in your life where friends or family stepped in to support you in a meaningful way?

Reflect on parts of your life where you're not being honest with yourself.

List problems in your life you have blamed others for in the past.

What are three areas in your life where you can improve your personal accountability?

ROCK BOTTOM WILL TEACH YOU LESSONS THAT MOUNTAIN TOPS NEVER WILL.

CHAPTER 2
HEALING PAST TRAUMA

Hardships often prepare ordinary people
for an extraordinary destiny.
- C.S. Lewis

What is a normal childhood? Most people think it's the representation you see in the movies with two parents, two kids and a dog. They grow up in a suburban neighborhood where they get into little scrapes, but for the most part, no one ends up in too much trouble. School Monday through Friday, movies on Saturday and church on Sunday. Family vacations, picnics and soccer games.

A "normal childhood" is a myth that many of us hold on to, but reality is never like it is on television or the big screen. Sometimes people do grow up in some kind of approximation of that myth, but there are always some pieces that are out of place. It might be a parent that works all the time and is never home, family financial struggles, tragic deaths, addiction, or any number of other things that are outside of what we consider ideal.

What we all have to work to understand is these imperfections in your normal childhood are not a handicap in your adult life. At least they don't have to be. You can recode yourself by doing the work of unlocking how those childhood experiences are affecting your adult actions. Pulling apart the tangle of past years of your life can be transformative. It was for me.

I really did think that my childhood was normal. It wasn't until I was in my thirties that I realized just how complicated and unusual my upbringing was. I want to be clear that I hold no ill will towards my parents or my siblings, that's not what revisiting the past is about. I don't feel that I was a child who suffered from abuse or neglect at the hands of anyone. Just like everyone, my childhood was complex. While there isn't a "normal" definition of the perfect family, there is such a thing as an average or a traditional family, and mine certainly wasn't that. I didn't realize how different my upbringing was or how it impacted the adult I had become until over a decade after I left home. Like most of us, I just buried my past. I wrestled with it in the dark of the night when I couldn't sleep, or at the bottom of a bottle of vodka that dulled my emotional pain.

Through many years of self-examination, I have figured out that even with my unusual upbringing, my issues are essentially the same as everyone else's. The good news is the work to realign myself is the same work you will need to do to heal your past trauma. Experiences that at the time seemed completely reasonable and logical to me, are now windows into my own self-limitations. No one is holding me back, but me.

I have come to learn it doesn't matter if what we experienced as kids was extreme or normal, it's all about perspective. Our subconscious minds create hurdles, so when you label your childhood as this or that you're coding your subconscious mind to put up barriers. Reading my story, many will see it as extreme, completely outside of what most people would consider to be normal. I invite you to focus on me as a real person, just like you, whose parents did their best to live good lives and give their kids the best opportunities available.

OUTSIDE FORCES

A lot of what shaped my family dynamics growing up was our religion, a form of conservative Christianity that placed hard rules on what was and was not permitted. Our family structure was not defined by my parents, but by the edicts of our faith. When I work to decode why my childhood was the way it was, it's impossible to unweave my family from the church.

FAMILY DYNAMICS

I grew up in a small house with tons of kids in it. When I was born, my mom and dad already had three other kids of their own, not including my much older half-sister that lived several states away. My dad worked hard, always trying to make ends meet and to feed and clothe everyone. My mom had been a hairdresser before she started having children. She stayed home with us for a while, but went back to work when I was still very young. I stayed at home with my Aunt Donna and those early, formative years shaped me a lot. There was a rare gap in children right before me, so I was raised as the oldest child in the house for a little while and that had a big influence on me.

My mother had nine children. Today that sounds like a lot, but try to remember that it was only a hundred years ago that everyone had that many kids. I know, it's not a hundred years ago, but that makes me feel a little better. My mom stayed pregnant for over a decade. I can't even imagine it. I was number four. Our family went Doyle, Benjamin, Ellen, me, Priscilla, William, Rulon, Richard, and then Mary. Everyone was just over a year apart, except for the gaps between Ellen and I and between Priscilla and William when my mother suffered miscarriages. Those gaps meant that I was five years younger than my older brother. The space is what made our relationship. Gender had a great deal of meaning in our religion, so being separated in birth order from my brothers meant that I was alone in many ways. Being closer in age to the girls wasn't an advantage. We couldn't share clothes because they dressed differently and there were very different expectations for girls and boys. Priscilla and I were the closest in age, but got along like oil and water due to gender and natural personality differences. Ellen tried to be my friend, stepping in when my older brothers rejected me, but the gender dissimilarity left a chasm. Boys were meant to be out roughhousing and girls inside playing with dolls. That left me feeling very alone in the middle of a large family.

It's bizarre to be alone in a family that size.

Our family dynamic isn't something that I resent. Looking back on it now, I can see how I was different from the rest of my family. Perhaps it was my differences that made me more of a loner, not them pushing me into isolation and making me feel like an outsider. I have come to realize it doesn't really matter.

The house felt very small, less than two thousand square feet with eleven people living in it. Because we were all so close in age, and because I was born in the middle, everyone was home for a large chunk of my childhood. We started off with four bedrooms, but as the family grew, we eventually added a fifth. There were two sets of bunk beds in each of our childhood bedrooms. We were always on top of each other, and I actually enjoyed sharing a bedroom with so many brothers. We spent very little time in the house, anyway, every chance we got we would run out the door and spend our days playing outside.

IMPORTANT MOMENTS

There are a few instances where I can look back at my childhood and clearly point to things that shaped me. Specific events prominent for not only my conscious mind, but that shaped my unconscious mind as well. The more time you spend reflecting on your childhood, the more of these moments you'll uncover. They're linked together like a web, interconnected to one another. This web continues to grow from the center of your life as a child out towards adulthood. Seemingly insignificant, everyday events that made up my childhood later manifested themselves in my adult life in surprising ways. Everyone experiences events that mold them in one way or another. It's how we react to these instances that is important and unique to our individual journeys.

Memories are not perfect, but science has revealed that memories tied to strong emotions leave the most indelible impressions on our minds. When you get that emotional hit in your gut, neurons connect to form long -term memories. The stronger the emotion, the stronger the memory.

In the big front yard of our small house, we had a large, beautiful willow tree. It's memorable because of its size and as the center of many of my childhood play experiences. My brothers and I would run around the tree and climb it, swing on the branches and sit under the shade of it to read when we were older. It was home base for games of hide and seek and we dug at the roots looking for bugs. I have strong positive associations with this tree for all of those reasons, because it was a happy place most of the time. For all of the grief that my brothers gave me, I continue to look to the wonderful memories.

Not all of my childhood associations with the willow tree were positive. With such a large family, the children were often unsupervised by adults for long periods of time. I was the younger, smaller boy and my older brothers often picked on me when they needed an outlet for their own frustrations. At times, they bullied me relentlessly, then would come back around and make nice later. Eager to be included, I always forgave them and even trusted them, naively.

One summer day, when I was about seven years old, my older brothers were up in the tree with some of the neighborhood kids. A gang of kids that you would expect to see in eighties movies like The Sandlot or Goonies. I needed a little help to climb up in the tree because I was smaller than the other children. I'd been reaching up and asking them to give me a hand, a little kid walking around and around the tree, leaping for the limbs and scraping my fingers against the bark. After a while, one of them said "Hey, I'll help you up here Tommy, just pull yourself up a little more."

I eagerly started scrambling against the tree, pushing up with my feet and pulling with my fingers. I looked down to find a better foothold when I felt a warm sensation falling over my head and down my shoulders. It was too warm to be rain, and I remember thinking I'm under the tree so it doesn't make sense that it would be raining. I couldn't fathom what it could possibly be until I looked up to see my older brother peeing on me, and the gang of boys all broke out into uncontrollable laughter.

It's a memory seared into my brain. The acrid smell of the urine soaking into my long sleeve shirt and the pitter-patter of the drops as they fell onto the hard-packed earth below me. The echo of the boys laughing. I don't remember what happened next, I must have gone into the house and told my mom or my Aunt Donna. I'm sure my older brothers got into some kind of trouble.

In many ways the willow tree was the center of my childhood. In its branches my brothers would push me to my limits. One day when I was about seven I was up in the tree with my brother who'd somehow acquired a pack of cigarettes. In those days cigarettes weren't as hard to come by because they were less expensive and less taboo than they are today. He dared me to smoke a cigarette. I was naturally curious about cigarettes because adults seemed so obsessed with them.

"Come on Thomas, don't be chicken," he said as he lit the end of the cigarette with a lighter and held it out to me.

"I don't know, what if I die from it?" I said.

"Quit being a wuss. Are you a baby? I knew you were nothing but a little baby."

I remember feeling scared but wanting more than anything to impress my brother, so I reached out and took the cigarette, desperate to please him and get his approval. I pulled the smoke into my lungs, and coughed so hard I felt like I was going to fall out of the tree. My brother laughed and egged me on. After a couple of puffs, my lungs were burning and my head was spinning. When I finished the cigarette he pushed me to keep going. I don't remember how many cigarettes I smoked in the willow tree that day, but I remember getting sick, puking on the dirt below.

My brothers seemed to enjoy tormenting me. When I was eight or nine my older brother got a BB gun for his birthday. I remember my dad said "You'll shoot your eye out" when he opened it. It was a big hit with the neighborhood kids. One day my brother found a piece of Styrofoam three or four inches thick from a shipping package.

"Ok Tommy, you hold this in front of your chest, and I'll shoot the BB gun at you. It'll work like a bullet proof vest. Don't worry, it won't get you. Look at how thick this foam is!"

"What if it does hit me?" I asked, trusting my big brother, but understandably nervous about his proposal.

"If it does hit you, then you can shoot the gun at me while I hold it. That's fair. It'll be really cool if you do it, and you'll show how brave you are. You are brave right? You're not some wussy little kid are you?"

I definitely didn't want to be a wussy little kid, I wanted to be like him big and strong, a man with a gun. So I held the Styrofoam in front of my chest and squinted my eyes as my brother aimed the gun at my chest.

Pow!

When the BB hit the foam, I staggered backwards and dropped my foam "vest". I looked down and saw a little hole in my shirt and a spot of red. The bb had gone right through the foam, through my shirt, and was embedded in the skin of my chest. I scraped at it with my fingernails and it popped out, but I was crying and upset. My brother was sympathetic at first, but then when it came time for me to shoot him, his tone changed.

"Oh look there wuss, it barely got you. There's no way I'm letting you shoot at me. You'd probably put my eye out."

He took his BB gun and went off to find some other poor kid to be his next victim, leaving me alone with a little hole in my chest. I still have the scar.

These are the kinds of stories that we hear and excuse by saying, "boys will be boys", and up to a point, that's true. Kids play and they play rough sometimes. When I look back at my childhood I see these experiences were laced with power dynamics. They were a major factor in molding me into who I've become and making me think that I'm not good enough, that I will never be good enough, to deserve unconditional love and acceptance. My insecurities fueled my feelings of inferiority and have motivated me to desperately seek acceptance from other people to validate myself throughout my adult life, because I felt that need wasn't met when I was a child.

Events in childhood plant a seed that grows within us, even when we don't acknowledge it. Some seeds can be incredibly positive, leading us to have joy in the unexpected or the courage to stay strong in the face of adversity. Others can lead us to the worst ends: addiction and suicide. I missed out on high school because I went to work when I was fourteen, but I learned how to work hard and I don't regret it. My parents were good people, and they did the best they could with their kids.

As an adult, when was the last time you really thought about your childhood and tried to process your different experiences? Most people just repress them. Some think that revisiting childhood trauma is a waste of time. I felt that way myself once, believing the past was in the past and that it didn't have any effect on my present or my future. I was wrong on both counts. Once I started peeling away the layers of paint I had used to cover my emotional cracks, it became crystal clear to me why I had made so many mistakes repeatedly throughout my life. I am convinced you need to understand where you come from to unlock the key to creating the present and future that you want.

Outline the structure of your family growing up.

What's a strong memory from your childhood that you feel shaped you?

CHAPTER 3
SELF-HONESTY

Feelings are just visitors. Let them come and go.
- Mooji

A lot of people see problems in their lives and immediately put the responsibility for their mistakes on someone else. Nothing is ever their fault. I've been that person and remained unable to accept personal accountability for many years. You've probably been this person too at some point in your life. Everyone I've ever known has gone through periods of transferring blame. Why do we do this? The answer is simple, it's a self-protection mechanism. It comes from our fear that if we face the reality of the mistakes we've made, that will somehow lessen our personal worth.

Emotionally healthy people are able to look at their mistakes and own them. They see mistakes as opportunities to grow and change, not failures. Some people are great at taking responsibility for making average-sized mistakes, for example being short-tempered with your spouse in an argument or cutting someone off on the freeway. These same people can have trouble owning big mistakes like addiction or other self-destructive behaviors. Lies are like snowballs, they grow until you feel you can't change who you've become.

Self-honesty can become a springboard helping you to jump into a better life. Only when you look at yourself and accept responsibility for everything you see and don't like, without putting the blame on anyone else, will you be able to move forward. Don't stay stuck in the blame game, it's a game no one wins.

THE PAST IS THE PAST

To progress you must learn to let go of the past. You've made mistakes and other people have made mistakes, you can't change either one. You also can't change the way people treat you today and in the future. The only thing you can control is your actions.

A lot of people blame their current problems on their childhood, saying "I had a rough time growing up, so it's my parent's fault that I'm doing these things today." No way. That's no excuse. You may have had a screwed up childhood, perhaps you were abused or abandoned. Maybe your religion made you fearful or poverty or disease limited your opportunities. You may have been persecuted because of your race or overlooked because of your gender. Along the way you learned coping mechanisms. All of the hard struggles you have endured have made you a survivor, or you wouldn't be here reading this book.

There are also a lot of people who didn't experience big childhood trauma. I don't think that I did, not anything close to what other people have endured. Everyone has hang-ups about what happened to them growing up, no matter how good their family was. We are all coded, and some of that coding is not going to work for you as an adult, it needs to be re-written.

What can you do to change your childhood? Nothing. You can't do a damn thing to change it. Try as you might, you don't have a time machine to go back and save your little self from whatever hurt was inflicted on you. This is also the case for everything that has happened to you up to this point in your adult life, including lost or abusive relationships. You can't change what's already happened.

So what can you do about painful, past experiences? Everything. You can change the way you look at them. You can take ownership for how they've affected your decisions. Most importantly, you can change the way that you live, based on this new understanding. The past is the past, but the present you and the future you can choose to act different- ly and not repeat old mistakes.

There is a lot of work to do when you're fixing yourself and changing old habits. It's not as simple as just "letting go of the past". You're taking an adult lens and looking back through your childhood at the events that caused you to be the way you are today. You can't just wave a magic wand and make past trauma disappear. If you run into a self-help program or a guru who promises to make this easier, run the other way as fast as you can. There is no path to a different fu- ture without deep and challenging reflections on your past. The good news is there is a kind of freedom on the other side, if you do the work. You won't be trapped by the events behind you forever.

DISHONESTY IN CHILDHOOD

One day when I was young a neighborhood kid asked me what re- ligion I practiced and I couldn't even say. I didn't know what our church was called or what the name of our religion was, but my par- ents had made it very clear that we weren't allowed to talk to anyone about our faith. People would ask us why we wore certain clothes, why there were so many kids in our family. We were taught to lie, but I didn't really understand what we were lying about.

As children, my siblings and I spent nearly all of our time outside. During the summer we'd ride our bikes all over the neighborhood and through the fields and trails behind our house. We weren't alone, the neighborhood was full of kids. We would all rummage for change then ride to the gas station about a mile away to buy bubble gum and soda. The neighbor children would always ask about our family, sometimes rudely, and my older brothers learned to be defensive and intimidating. The kids didn't bother them as much as they bothered me, because I was younger and less willing to fight.

I felt embarrassed and ashamed around people outside of our church, especially when I was out in public with my mother or sisters. The clothes we wore as boys looked a little different than the other neighborhood boys, but the girl's clothing was drastically different and they really stood out with their long skirts and braided hair. There was never a moment of real ease and comfort in my childhood; I was always on my toes watching how I acted at home and in public. This created a deep feeling of internal dishonesty because I never felt comfortable just being myself. I never figured out who I was, because I was constantly told who I had to be, and was subject to long lists of rules and regulations.

I can trace my personal difficulties with self-honesty back to fractures that happened in my childhood. When you're taught to lie about your reality from the time you can talk, you feel you have to wear a mask at all times. It becomes harder and harder to take that mask off. Everyone copes in different ways. My older brother ended up in prison for a total of sixteen years because he coped in negative ways.

Self-dishonesty doesn't happen only when you're in an extreme situation like I was growing up. The defenses you formed to cope as a child are still there in adulthood, covering up who you really are and warring with your inner self. Until you look back and figure out what those defenses are, and why they formed, you're not going to be able to embrace self-honesty or truly improve your life.

THE CRISIS OF MIDLIFE

A midlife crisis is an emotional identify and self-confidence transition that typically occurs in early middle age. Some people in their late forties or early fifties have extreme reactions to midlife, in some cases freaking out and trashing the work they've done up to that point in their lives. Long-term relationships are dumped, jobs are changed, and sports cars are purchased. The clichés are annoying, but the emotional pain is real.

Typically, the reason people have a midlife crisis is because they haven't dealt with trauma in their childhood and it finally catches up with them. If you've willed yourself to think that you've moved on and healed, but you've really only repressed those experiences, they will come back to haunt you.

As I aged, I started to feel that I'd never been steering my own ship. The choices I'd made, suddenly didn't feel like choices anymore. Where did those ideas come from? Why did I go to college or not go to college? Why did I end up in this job and not that job? Why did I marry this person and not another? My life started to feel suffocating when I believed I had very little control over my life choices. This led to my midlife crisis and ultimately major change.

To get through it, I just went with the flow, and that made me unhappy. Then I turned to some kind of addiction to numb my feelings. It's different for everyone, it might be social media, drugs, sex, TV, gambling, the list of possible distractions is long. All addiction is an escape from reality, but some forms are more destructive than others. I didn't dare try honesty and facing my challenges, that was just not on the table for me at the time because it felt too terrifying. In all honesty I didn't know where the problem stemmed from or how to even attempt to fix it. For years drinking and avoidance were my coping mechanisms and I was in denial that they weren't working for me.

Hypnotherapy opened doors for me. I discovered I had abandonment issues, something I would never have figured out on my own. During the out-of-control times in my life, before I found my own path to deal with my past, I could never escape my childhood trauma. It controlled me from the inside out. I was afraid to deal with what was behind me, and I thought it would only get better if I pushed it down. Hypnotherapy allowed me to look inward, without the baggage that kept me from seeing things honestly. It's not something I could have done before midlife. Maturity and life experience played a key role in my process. I couldn't be honest with myself until I had been through some of the fires of life.

I believe everyone has the potential to come to terms with their childhood traumas. A young, new wife or fancy, fast car won't redefine you and giving in to depression or addiction can kill you. Your subconscious won't let the past go, it can't let it go without you doing the work to integrate it into your present. The past never leaves you, not even when you have done the hard work to get through it, but your daily life can be free from your painful past experiences. Your past does not control your future.

MOMENTS OF CLARITY

Routine is human nature, and that can be both good and bad. Once you get into a cycle, it can feel impossible to break away from old habits. You come back for more of whatever remedy seems to be working at the moment. Leading up to my turning point, I was in a routine of getting up in the morning hungover, going to work and suffering through the day, then heading home to drink again and pass out until the morning only to start the cycle all over again. I worked for the weekend and any time off I could manage, so I could drink more alcohol than anyone should. I made poor and dangerous decisions when I was in an impaired state.

I was able to break this self-destructive cycle when self-honesty led me to a moment of extreme clarity and a subconscious realization. For me, a change of scenery led to my first big realization. Somehow, despite all my drinking, I managed to continue earning good money during the darkest period of my life. Extremely good money. I was driving a Porsche and had a bank account full of money. I'll never know how I was able to keep getting paid like that going to work hungover every day, but my financial success fed into my self-delusion that I was doing fine and I could control my drinking. I would receive these huge checks, fifty or sixty thousand dollars at a time, so I built a house, bought a fast car and spent irresponsibly, just because I could.

About a year before my suicide attempt, I had some time off work around midsummer, in late June. I'd just earned a large commission at work, and on a whim I decided to go to London. I literally called the airport, booked the flight and was in the air all within three hours. For four days in London, I didn't drink, not one sip of alcohol. Partly because I didn't know the city at all and was pretty terrified of getting into trouble away from my home country. One thing I'd always steered clear of was jail time; that had been a strict boundary for me. I realized at home my drinking had gotten bad, and this overseas trip gave me a chance to leave my addiction behind for a few days. London was a way for me to put up a boundary for myself. It wasn't easy, because of the level that I'd been drinking I spent four painful days withdrawing from alcohol, but it was worth it. With my mind and body free from the drug, I felt like I'd earned a whole new lease on life. On the plane ride home, the flight attendant offered me a drink and I turned her down. I thought I could just stop cold turkey, just like that. I felt empowered and told myself that this was it, I would finally be done with alcohol.

Unfortunately, it wasn't that easy. Old habits die hard. When you're changing your life, you can't make sweeping changes without putting a support system into place. I thought that I could fly off to another continent and come back to a new life. But when I walked in my front door and dropped my bag, there on the kitchen counter sat a half-full bottle of vodka and the cycle started all over again. Why? I hadn't broken my old code. I'd only put a temporary patch on a much larger problem for four days in London.

ALWAYS POSITIVE

I wasn't always a positive person. Prior to the suicide attempt, I was a man who struggled to see the good in the world. After that wake-up call, things changed drastically for me. Now I hear the same questions all the time, and I have to say that it's a better place to be in than where I was before. People ask me:

"How can you be so positive all the time?"

"Don't you ever have a bad day, Thomas?"

"Why aren't you angrier about your past?"

I tell people that I choose to be positive. Even when life is at its worst, you have to plant seeds of goodness in your life or you'll grow a tree of doom. The smallest thoughts of positivity grow into something bigger, with each passing day. Positivity is a choice that you make in moments that challenge you. You can choose to look for the good in the world around you, even when your life seems to be falling apart.

Now before you start thinking this is some corny self-help bullshit, hear me out. Who talks to you the most? You do. No one in your life past, present or future has as much influence on your thinking as you do. Your world is your own creation. This isn't a point of view, it's a fact. The only person who is with you from the moment you're born until the moment you die, is you. Think about that.

If you extend this truth out, then you start to realize that the only person whose opinion should matter to you in life, is yours. Not your parents, or your siblings, not your faith leaders, or your teachers, not your boss, or your spouse and kids. Though you might have obligations and important responsibilities to other people, at the end of the day, you are the most important person in your life. If you decide to drink yourself into oblivion like I did, it's you who will suffer the most. If you decide to pack up and fly to London to reset yourself, like I did, or make a permanent physical move, you'll still be stuck with your old self when you get there. All of the pressures and habits you want to escape are real, but they aren't permanent.

As a parent or a partner in a relationship, it may seem selfish to put yourself in the center of your life. It's not. Think about how you would want your child to live. Do you want them to put someone else's needs ahead of their own, or do you want them to find self-fulfillment independent of anyone else? You deserve the same.

Your life isn't going to get better until you change how you think, until you turn towards the positive. Your family can't help you. Your partner can't fix you. Your love for your children won't transform you. This book is not going to save you. You're on your own. This radical self-honesty may sound harsh, but it's the path to true mental and emotional freedom.

How has your past shaped your present? Name two things from your past that you're carrying with you every day that affects your life.

Choose one childhood or formative experience and look at it from a different angle with the goal to see it as a positive thing in your life.

Think about how you talk to yourself. Is your inner voice leaning positive or negative?

CHAPTER 4
IDENTIFYING TRUE DESIRES

Fears and insecurities are unconsciously created by you.
If you do not create them, they do not exist.
- Sadhguru

When you start off in life, you usually begin with your parents telling you what to do and where to go. They decide what church you attend, the school you go to, your friends, and what things you're exposed to. Your family controls you. That's not always a bad thing, in a lot of ways parenting is about guiding children toward making the right choices. The problem is that no parent is perfect, including me. As parents we unintentionally pass on positive and negative traits to our kids.

Layer after layer builds up throughout childhood, hiding who you really are. Unless we consciously work against it, our true desires become hidden deep under the expectations and habits of our formative years. Beneath the layers of coding we were programmed with.

We know from social science that, for the most part, our life paths are decided for us. If you're born into a middle-class, Presbyterian family, and your parents had bachelor's degrees, then you'll likely to grow up to me a middle-class Presbyterian with a bachelor's degree. If your parents both had doctorates from Ivy League schools and made six-figure salaries, you're more likely to follow in their footsteps. If your family is full of relatives who struggled with drug addiction and got mixed up in the prison system, you're likely to go down that same path. The American dream involves breaking out of that pattern, but it's honestly kind of a pipe dream for most people. If you want to change your life, you have to look at the childhood programming that coded them to end up where they are in life.

Society tells us your socio-economic background doesn't matter, you can have the American dream if you work hard enough. The truth is no one accidentally breaks out of the coding that they started with, it only happens with a lot of hard work and intention.

UNRAVELING YOURSELF

I know firsthand what a challenge it is to feel like your adult actions are the product of forces outside of yourself, like your childhood upbringing and family dynamics. The thing that will save you is letting go of your fear of getting to the root of the truth. It won't happen in an instant and it won't be easy, but it's a goal that you can work towards every day. Instead of just putting your head down and ignoring reality, you need to unravel your perceived reality to uncover the truth. I use the word unravel because it is like pulling apart a knitted sweater or untying a tangle of knotted rope. At first, it may seem impossible and it will take a long time, but when you come out on the other side you'll have this neat, long piece of straight fibers that you can create whatever you want your life to be, free from the form that you were forced into.

I didn't realize how much of my adult self was wrapped up in my childhood until I was much older. I arrived at where I am now by digging deep into my family history with. The most striking thing that I learned was that my family didn't intend to hurt me. They weren't monsters who were out to make my life hard or to screw me up, they were good people who loved me struggling through their own tough times and dealing with their own coding limitations. One thing you learn on this journey is that being mad at someone, especially your family, won't help you at all. It might feel vindicating for a little while, but the anger doesn't punish or hurt anyone except yourself.

I started my unraveling process by tracing back the origin of my obvious, big problems like alcoholism, but as I kept untangling, I realized even little habits that negatively impacted my daily life could be traced back to childhood traumas. The rabbit hole is deep when you start going down it, and for me it went back not just to the influence of my parents, but to Chapter 4 Identifying True Desires

---

**FEARS AND INSECURITIES ARE
UNCONSCIOUSLY CREATED BY YOU.
IF YOU DO NOT CREATE THEM,
THEY DO NOT EXIST.**

- Sadhguru

When you start off in life, you usually begin with your parents telling you what to do and where to go. They decide what church you attend, the school you go to, your friends, and what things you're exposed to. Your family controls you. That's not always a bad thing, in a lot of ways parenting is about guiding children toward making the right choices. The problem is that no parent is perfect, including me. As parents we unintentionally pass on positive and negative traits to our kids.

Layer after layer builds up throughout childhood, hiding who you really are. Unless we consciously work against it, our true desires become hidden deep under the expectations and habits of our formative years. Beneath the layers of coding we were programmed with.

We know from social science that, for the most part, our life paths are decided for us. If you're born into a middle-class, Presbyterian family, and your parents had bachelor's degrees, then you'll likely to grow up to me a middle-class Presbyterian with a bachelor's degree. If your parents both had doctorates from Ivy League schools and made six-figure salaries, you're more likely to follow in their footsteps. If your family is full of relatives who struggled with drug addiction and got mixed up in the prison system, you're likely to go down that same path. The American dream involves breaking out of that pattern, but it's honestly kind of a pipe dream for most people. If you want to change your life, you have to look at the childhood programming that coded them to end up where they are in life.

Society tells us your socio-economic background doesn't matter, you can have the American dream if you work hard enough. The truth is no one accidentally breaks out of the coding that they started with, it only happens with a lot of hard work and intention.

UNRAVELING YOURSELF

I know firsthand what a challenge it is to feel like your adult actions are the product of forces outside of yourself, like your childhood upbringing and family dynamics. The thing that will save you is letting go of your fear of getting to the root of the truth. It won't happen in an instant and it won't be easy, but it's a goal that you can work towards every day. Instead of just putting your head down and ignoring reality, you need to unravel your perceived reality to uncover the truth. I use the word unravel because it is like pulling apart a knitted sweater or untying a tangle of knotted rope. At first, it may seem impossible and it will take a long time, but when you come out on the other side you'll have this neat, long piece of straight fibers that you can create whatever you want your life to be, free from the form that you were forced into.

I didn't realize how much of my adult self was wrapped up in my childhood until I was much older. I arrived at where I am now by digging deep into my family history with. The most striking thing that I learned was that my family didn't intend to hurt me. They weren't monsters who were out to make my life hard or to screw me up, they were good people who loved me struggling through their own tough times and dealing with their own coding limitations. One thing you learn on this journey is that being mad at someone, especially your family, won't help you at all. It might feel vindicating for a little while, but the anger doesn't punish or hurt anyone except yourself.

I started my unraveling process by tracing back the origin of my obvious, big problems like alcoholism, but as I kept untangling, I realized even little habits that negatively impacted my daily life could be traced back to childhood traumas. The rabbit hole is deep when you start going down it, and for me it went back not just to the influence of my parents, but to grandparents and great grandparents too. The deeper you look, the more you deepen your understanding of yourself. You also start to understand how your life is part of a wider web that influenced you, extending out to, your family but also the community that shaped your life.

Now I'm the total opposite. I can't stand people who lie, and I can't stand to lie myself, not even about little things. The absolute worst feeling for me is to know in the pit of my stomach that I'm not being truthful. What's just as much of an impact on me today is that I believe that everyone else is lying to me, all the time. My trust in outside appearances was so broken from those childhood experiences that I struggle to believe anyone. It is hard to find honest people in the world, but I also recognize that my almost paranoia about people being dishonest has less to do with them lying than it does to do with my upbringing in a world full of smoke and mirrors.

GENERATIONAL HABITS AND HANG-UPS

Even though I feel like I had a pretty stable childhood, there was a lot of instability wrapped up in the secrecy and lies surrounding my family. I was taught not to trust anyone, and this made me feel isolated and unstable. There were lots of things in my childhood that were very confusing. I felt like I never understood what was going on.

My parents were very protective, to the point of being controlling. I was raised similarly to the other kids of my faith, we attended a church-run school and all of my friends had parents who dictated a lot in their lives. Growing up, I was never allowed to have sleepovers with other kids. I wasn't allowed to go into their homes to play. I wasn't allowed to go off to events with other families, not even other families from our church my family knew well. The neighborhood children could come play at our house or we could play together outside, but we couldn't be alone with anyone at their homes. I made excuses for it and learned to lie from a really young age. An age where kids shouldn't have to lie to anyone about anything. I would tell a friend that I didn't want to stay over at their house because I didn't like being away from home or I had something to do the next day. The truth was that my mom would never allow it, I was never told the reason, instead, I was taught to lie. Feeling that I had to lie as a kid to people I wanted so much to fit in with, was tough on me, even at the time.

This was one of the things that I didn't realize was weird until I was much older. I figured that my mom not allowing me to hang out with friends at their homes was just one of those things. Like wearing long pants all the time and not listening to secular music.

It wasn't until I was an adult that I figured out the real reason that I could never go play with other kids. It had to do with my Mom's coding. She was molested when she was a child, her sister too. It's something she never told us when we were kids, and something she still doesn't like to talk about now, for obvious reasons. Her decision to never let us be alone with other families was directly related to her childhood trauma. It makes sense to me now I know the truth. Knowing this fact about her history explains a lot of things, including why she chose to raise her family in a strict, tight-knit religious community. It felt like another layer of protection to keep the same kind of horrible thing from happening to her children.

Knowing why I was raised the way I was changes my relationship with both my mom and my own child. Is it ok to let a child go have a playdate with a trusted family? Yes, of course it is. I know why my mother held on so tight to me, but that doesn't mean I have to follow in her exact footsteps. I can identify what is right for my family and parent in my own way.

PASSING ON VICES

Vices, whether they're addictions, negative relationships, or the mishandling of money are central tenants that get passed down from generation to generation. The encouraging news is that just like your parents can pass on a vice to you, you can consciously choose not to pass on those vices to the next generation, thereby ending the cycle.

We don't always realize that our problems were inherited from the generations before us. Alcohol was strictly forbidden in the Church I grew up in and drinking even the smallest bit of beer or wine was considered a major sin. Because my parents raised me in this very strict religion, I never saw anyone drinking alcohol when I was a kid and I couldn't fathom my parents drinking. Because of my upbringing, I thought that my alcoholism was a vice that just plagued me and started with me.

The close-knit nature of my family and my church was one of the reasons it was such a shock for me to find out that my dad had been a closet alcoholic my entire life. Before he moved back to Utah with my mom to join the FLDS Church, he'd run a printing company in New Mexico with my grandmother. In Utah, he got a job with another printing press publishing magazines and advertisements. The job involved long hours and lots of overtime. He also had church commitments that added to his stressful weekly workload. I remember my dad always had a coffee thermos that he drank out of, constantly. It went with him everywhere. When I grew up, long after I'd developed a serious drinking problem myself, I learned from my sister that the thermos didn't have coffee in it, it was my father's way of concealing his alcohol. My dad was a functioning alcoholic holding down a job and raising a family, just like me. I never had any idea my dad was struggling with an addiction and coped exactly the same way that I ended up functioning as an adult. Later in my life I learned his mother, my paternal grandmother, had the same struggle with addiction. Her choice of alcohol was also vodka. I am determined to be honest with my son about our family's history of addiction in an effort to break the cycle of silence and alcoholism.

This is one example of how generational vices are passed down through families. You may not have similar mirrors between you and your parents or grandparents, but you definitely have some shadows of their behavior that run through your life. Your job is to uncover what those influences are, how they impact your life, and whether or not you want to pass them on to the next generation. When you're able to trace the origins of your behaviors, a lot of what you're experiencing in life will start to make sense. It's a portion of my family life that I look back on now with total disbelief.

When I left the FLDS Church as an adult, I explored all kinds of things that had previously been off limits to me: women, alcohol, etc. Not only things that are normally off limits to teenagers, I grew up in a religion where members were forbidden from wearing the color red or growing a mustache, these were "sins" that could condemn you to hell. We weren't allowed to listen to popular music or read books not approved by the church. When I left, I indulged in everything previously forbidden. I bought red clothes and wore them. I went out to places where pop music played and I drank at bars. I grew facial hair and stopped attending Sunday church services. To me, all of these "sins" were weighed equally by God. It was just as wicked for me to put on a bright red t-shirt as it was for me to sleep with a woman that I wasn't married to. This strict code of conduct originating from the church I had grown up in influenced my ideas about what was normal and right or wrong. Echoes of this mindset still stay with me today and are issues that I continue to work through.

YOUR PAST IS NOT YOUR TRUTH

It doesn't matter what form it takes, your family is always going to have a central role in your life. It should, but in a healthy way.

Some people choose to stay connected with the family they were born into, others create a non-traditional family unit comprised of close friends and like-minded people. Regardless of your family structure, your habits and vices are shaped by the people you surround yourself with. It can be a good thing or a bad thing, depending on your family dynamic, but it's always going to be a factor.

Whoever you're surrounding yourself with is going to rub off on you. For many of us, family ends up defining truth in our lives, this should never be the case. Even if your family is wonderful, the only person that should define your life is you. Figure out who you are, what you want, and what you don't want in your life. Instead of going along with your life like you always have without thinking about it, take a critical look at it your habits and vices and dissect what is really motivating these behaviors.

When you identify what's holding you back and what baggage from the past you're bringing into your present day decisions, you're on the path to finding out what your true desires are. It's not until you look back, that you can look forward.

What negative coding are you carrying with you from your upbringing? Come up with at least one example.

What are the vices that you want to change the most? Don't list more than three.

PART II - CONDITIONING

UNTIL YOU CHANGE
YOUR THINKING,
YOU WILL ALWAYS
RECYCLE YOUR
EXPERIENCES.

CHAPTER 5
EXTERNAL INFLUENCES

Man cannot live without joy;
therefore when he is deprived of true spiritual joys
it is necessary that he become
addicted to carnal pleasures.
- Thomas Aquinas

Things aren't always what they seem. If there's anything that I've learned from my experiences it's that secrets live in even the most seemingly honest of places. I'm going to share more of my personal history and how understanding the external influences that pressed on me influenced me in the hope that you'll start to get a better feeling for the external influences that are pressing on you.

LIFE UNDER THE PROPHET

I grew up in a religion that I now feel was more cult than faith. The FLDS Church is a group that believes in modern-day prophets who rule over a flock of followers that adhere to the belief that the only way to save your eternal soul is to obey the prophet's teachings to the letter of the law. To the people in the church, the prophets have a direct line from God's mouth to their ears. These men (only men can be prophets in the FLDS Church) were revered as the ultimate source of information from the Divine. Sometimes these teachings go off the rails, and people are asked to do things that seem extreme, especially to people outside of the church. The more extreme the dogma the more difficult it was to control the member's behavior. This trend was something I personally experienced in the FLDS Church as the prophet tried to control his followers more with every passing year.

Now for a brief history lesson. The Fundamentalist Church of Jesus Christ of Latter-Day Saints (FLDS Church) is an offshoot of the Church of Jesus Christ of Latter-day Saints (LDS), popularly known as the Mormon Church. For readers who have never heard of either, to simplify they're both basically modern churches practicing Christianity that believe in the Bible but also believe that Jesus visited the American continent after his death in 33 AD, recorded in a second book of scripture called the Book of Mormon. These revelations came through a man called Joseph Smith in the early 1800's. Early members of the LDS Church were persecuted and driven west in search of a place where they could practice their religion in peace, eventually settling Utah. Here the LDS church flourished, but some of the more controversial practices instituted by Smith, like polygamy, were abandoned by the LDS Church because they were illegal in the United States and prevented Utah from acquiring statehood.

The FLDS split off from the LDS church in the early 20th Century because a faction of followers believed that the LDS church had strayed too far from the original teachings of the first prophet Joseph Smith. The split boiled down to one key issue: polygamy.

Joseph Smith had as many as 40 wives. Brigham Young, who took over as prophet of the LDS church after Smith died, had fifty-five wives. Having more than one wife was a calling for the men in the Mormon Church, not a lifestyle choice, but a tenant of the religion that would qualify participants for exaltation in heaven. Similar to the practice of confession in the Catholic Church or the important bar mitzvah ceremony for people practicing Judaism. There was a deep belief among those early pioneers of the LDS Church that having multiple wives was the key to admittance into heaven. For both men and women, this was a commandment from God. Polygamy was illegal in the United States at the time and so church members were torn between complying with the law of the land or obeying God's law. Many who continued to practice polygamy were imprisoned and separated from their wives and children, splitting up families. So the mainstream Mormon Church officially ended the practice of polygamy but some church members continued to practice polygamy secretly and in 1930 the FLDS faction split off from the LDS church officially and members were excommunicated because they refused to renounce polygamy.

There were lots of break offs in the early days of the LDS Church, so the FLDS church's early history is fuzzy.

In 1953 the Arizona National Guard raided the community of Short Creek where the FLDS church was centered at the time, seizing over two hundred children and breaking up families. It's still the largest mass arrest of polygamists in America's history and created a deep sense of distrust between church leaders and local authorities that continues today. The 1953 raid directly influenced my family and life because my grandfather's four wives fled to four different parts of the country to avoid arrest and keep their families together.

A tenet of the FLDS Church unique from most religions is the idea the prophet makes all of the major decisions for the congregants. The prophet in 1986 was Rulon Jeffs after Leroy Johnson died and then went on with his son Warren Jeffs. The Jeffs were the leaders of the FLDS Church that I personally knew. During Rulon's leadership, the prophet would get revelation from God and would communicate it to the people, making rules that controlled everything from the way we prayed to how much money we gave the church. It was an all-or-nothing religion when I was growing up FLDS, you had to follow every tenet exactly or you were pushed out.

HARD HANDED RULERS

You've got to understand that growing up in a religious community like this is totally unlike how other people grow up. In a normal family, a mother and father make decisions pretty much on their own without outside interference. In the FLDS Church, the mother definitely doesn't have a say and the father has very little decision-making authority. The church dictates all aspects of family life, from where you live, to who you marry.

That's right, in my church no one got to choose who they married. The prophet chose who you married and how many women were married to one man. He also had the authority to dissolve marriages if a man was kicked out of the church. If a man did something wrong, or was seen as a threat to the prophet's power, his wives and children were assigned to another man and he'd be forced to leave the church. I saw this happen to families and it was especially tough on the kids. With ten kids and only two wives my dad had a small family compared to our neighbors. We were never considered a prominent family in the group and were fortunate to fly under the radar insulated from the prophet's wrath.

In the 1950's when my paternal grandfather had to split up his four wives because of the government raid, he sent one of his four families to Arizona. My father and his full-blood siblings went with my grandmother and created a life separate from the FLDS Church. They broke with their faith and didn't follow the strict rules anymore, so my dad spent a large chunk of his childhood outside the FLDS Church. Eventually he met and married my mom and they decided to rejoin the FLDS Church after they'd had a couple of kids. I believe their motivation was to raise their family in a stable, structured environment. Because my father and mother had chosen each other instead of having their marriage forced on them, it marked us as different in the FLDS Church.

For his second wife, my father wasn't given a choice and neither was my mother. My mother's sister Donna decided to move to Utah to join the FLDS Church. The prophet at the time wanted to find a husband for her and he chose my dad. So, my mom's sister became my father's second wife. In public we called her Aunt Donna, but at home and at church we called her Mama Donna.

Donna and my Dad only had one child together, a daughter. That made a total of ten children in our family's home. It was actually not confusing for us to have my aunt as my father's second wife, but looking back I can see how it really changed our family. My older brothers were probably more affected by it than I was because they would have remembered better the time before she came to live with us. Growing up, most of the families that we knew had multiple wives, and it wasn't uncommon to have sisters that were married to the same man. It was a little weird, I guess, but no one made a big deal about it so we didn't either.

The second marriage was a strain for my mom because she had never been close to her sister, and they didn't get along as sister wives either. It created turmoil in our house whenever we all had to interact together, which is probably another reason that the kids spent so much time outside. Even though we all lived in the same house, I didn't see a whole lot of Donna. My father and my mother had chosen to be together, but they didn't get to choose this addition to our family. It's still strange for me to imagine how people allow someone else to dictate something like their spouse to them. I knew as a kid that it would happen to me one day, because as a child I accepted the rule of the prophet. Now that seems like a long time ago when I was a very different person.

THE SHROUD OF SECRECY

The hard and fast rule in our family and the FLDS community was that everyone had to keep polygamy a secret. Remember, the way we lived was against the law. Aunt Donna was presented to the outside world as my mom's sister who lived with us. To the public, her daughter wasn't my sister, even though that's how we lived at home. The code of silence was emphasized more to me than anything else as a child. We lived in absolute fear of what would happen if the outside world learned our secret.

There were secrets everywhere. No one really knew what was going on with the inner workings of the church. Imagine rings of protection around the prophet and his closest relatives. The closer you got to the prophet, the more bizarre and controlling things became. Decisions about where we would live and who we would marry came down as decrees from inside the church's leadership. We didn't know how decisions were made or who made them, we weren't allowed to question and were conditioned to obey or be punished.

Interactions with the outside world were strictly prohibited for FLDS Church members. Listening to secular music and watching movies wasn't allowed. You couldn't talk to people outside the church, and FLDS children certainly weren't allowed to go to public schools. All of the children were educated at home if they lived outside the FLDS community or at the church-run school. I attended the FLDS Church school from kindergarten through high school and during that time Warren Jeffs was the principal. He had a way of interacting with us as students that made you both fear and revere him. To us, Jeffs was a holy man, the prophet and someone who walked close to God.

My initial impressions of Jeffs were not good, he always gave me a creepy, odd feeling. Even as a young child, I had a sense that something was not right with him. It was this uneasy dichotomy of not feeling comfortable with him but wanting his approval because of his status in the church that conflicted me growing up.

I distinctly remember one instance in fourth grade shortly after my mom had cut my hair at home. She had worked as a hairdresser before marrying my dad and knew what she was doing. I was called from the classroom upstairs to Jeff's office, a room with wood paneling and a ceiling that angled with the gable of the roof. The odd angles made the room feel tight, like you were right in the prophet's face and couldn't escape from him. My teacher had sent me to the principal's office to get a piece of candy because I'd been "caught being good". There were several children that went to the principal's office together; we stood in a long line and went into the office one at a time. When it was my turn I went in the room with Jeffs and he complimented me on what a good job I'd done being obedient in class and he handed me a piece of candy. It felt good to be complimented by someone with his power and as I turned to walk out, I felt this great boost of confidence like I was king of the world.

Then Jeffs stopped me and said "Who cut your hair Thomas?" I told him my mom had. "Well it's too short in the back and you're out of compliance with the dress code. Make sure you let your mother know I said so."

I went from feeling ten feet tall to feeling like an ant beneath a boot. Going from an extreme high to a devastating low like that happened a lot with Jeffs. He'd pull you up and make you feel good, only to snatch that away from you and make you feel small again. This cycle breaks your spirit, especially as a child. We were ingrained with the idea that the most important thing we needed to do in or lives was to please the prophet. Now that I'm an adult and have researched motivation I realize this was a control tactic Jeffs employed to keep his followers dependent on him.

DEPENDENCE VS. INDEPENDENCE

Those early experiences with the external influences of the FLDS Church have taking orders. I have a hard time accepting that what someone is asking me to do is something that I should be doing.

This is a sentiment you can probably relate to even if you weren't raised in a cult, like I was. Childhood trust is easily broken, and those early experiences change how we view the world. If someone, whether it's a cult leader like Warren Jeffs or an abusive parent, breaks your spirit during your formative years you can become deeply distrustful of people. It's not something that you can just piece back together. From my own perspective and based on my personal experience, I don't think that you can ever really fix it. You work through your issues and move on with your life learning to trust again, but you can't regain the innocence of childhood when it's taken away. It can affect every aspect of adult life and all relationships including work and family.

There are positive aspects that have come out of my childhood trauma that I see in myself. I have become a survivor in ways that help me to be successful today. These positive takeaways have come after years of dissecting the coding the FLDS Church programed into me. Initially, after leaving the FLDS Church I refused to take anyone's advice. I struggled to recognize any type of authority figure, even when they treated me well. Some of this bled into my work ethic, I learned to become self-motivated instead of doing tasks because a powerful person told me to. There is much more meaning and fulfillment when it's your choice, and you do a better job when it's on your terms. I've discovered that it's impossible to be fully satisfied if you are only making your way in life because you're told to.

When you are being controlled by something outside of yourself, there's a sense of safety and comfort in that. If bad things happen it's not your fault because you were following the rules. The person who is guiding you might tell you to do the wrong thing or an immoral thing, but you don't feel guilty because it wasn't really your fault. The upside of not being in a cult anymore was learning to take personal responsibility for my actions. I accepted that all of my problems weren't the fault of the FLDS. At this point in my life, I've nearly been out of the FLDS Church longer than I was in it. I've realized that I can't continue to blame other people for what I'm doing to myself. Not even Warren Jeffs.

Name something from your past that you were told to lie about when you were a child.

How did rules shape your life growing up? How do they continue to shape it now?

CHAPTER 6
OBEDIENCE

If you let a person talk long enough, you'll
hear their true intentions. Listen twice, speak once.
- Tupac

There is a fable that says if you drop a frog into a pot of boiling water it will jump out as soon as it hits the hot water. That same frog in a pot of cool water slowly heated to a boil won't know that it's in danger until it's too late to escape.

This is similar to how the FLDS Church maintained control over its members. The church didn't start out by exercising extreme control, they began by issuing rules that seemed completely reasonable. There were never edicts so dramatic that they would cause members of the church to question, "What's going on here? That seems extreme." Instead the rules and restrictions slowly built over time until they became unthinkable.

TURNING UP THE HEAT

Here's an illustration that I saw in my own family. The standard tithe that Christians are supposed to donate, across the board, no matter what denomination you're in, is ten percent. That number is biblical, it comes from the Old Testament. The Mormon Church uses this same number, just like the Catholic Church and pretty much every other Christian denomination. It is expected that members of these churches will voluntary donate ten percent of their increase, but no one comes to your home and forces you to give money to your church in those denominations, they're not checking your bank account to verify you are paying an honest tithe.

In the FLDS Church every man, because men were always in charge of the family's money, was required to give ten percent of his income to support the church. That standard is not excessive. The community was small, so if you didn't donate your ten percent you were shamed by other church members who were your neighbors. There are other small religious groups that employ similar tactics and it makes sense that a small congregation would need funds from each member family to help the church function. Challenges in the FLDS Church arose when the prophet would say something like "We need an extra five hundred dollars this month from every family to help fund the school." Edicts like that were understandable because a school is a community resource that we all used. Then a few months later the prophet would say "The roof on the meeting house needs to be replaced before the winter, we'll need an extra seven hundred dollars from every family this month to pay for it." This also seemed reasonable because we didn't want our house of worship falling in on us. Then not long after, "We'll need an extra fifteen hundred dollars this month from every family to pay legal fees to fight the government's prosecution of our church." That's a little more extreme, a tougher sell, but our FLDS community had a history of government intrusion and were conditioned to making sacrifices for our faith. My father wrote the check and our family ate a little less, but we were still ok. Then the edict became "We need each family to pay an extra five hundred dollars every month over your ten percent tithe to support the church." By the time this was the decree from the church leadership we'd already given over ten percent many times and were conditioned to being asked to sacrifice. I remember we were actually thankful that they were only asking for five hundred and not an extra fifteen hundred dollars every month. That number continued to increase, slowly, over a period of years until we were paying a third and then half of our income to the church. Just like the frog on the stove, we were slowly being boiled to death and didn't recognize it because our financial freedom was being eroded so subtly.

The FLDS Church is very secretive, so they don't disclose how much money they have in the bank. Through police investigations we know the church, not its members, own over one hundred fifteen million dollars in property, including seven hundred and fifty homes. That's another method of control employed by FLDS leaders, because church members live in houses they don't own. If a family fell out of favor with the Prophet, he could evict them or if they were in his good graces the family would be rewarded with a larger house. That's something that happened too, because the church was in total control. At first it seemed like a good thing because you got this bigger, better house, but then it also pulled you in deeper and put them more in control.

THE CHURCH IS ALWAYS RIGHT

You're taught in the church, from a very young age, that the people in charge know everything and that they're always right. It quickly becomes blindly following them. If they came out with a new edict, you just did it. Then what happens if things in your life aren't working? What if your marriage is miserable or your kids were acting out It couldn't possibly be the fault of the church, because the prophet is always right? That only left you to be at fault, so the guilt of everything in your life becomes heaped on top of you. All good things flow from the faith, all the bad things from the individual. You get to a point where you believe in this so heavily that you distrust yourself. It's brainwashing technique that keeps you from thinking for yourself.

Growing up in this church, I was never confident in anything that I did. I would constantly change my path, in an attempt to get to a place more in line with the teachings of the Prophet because I wanted so desperately to be a good and righteous person. This is one method of control for a religion like the FLDS, they want followers to be dependent on them and deeply distrusting of themselves and other people. The church must be the only source of truth or they feared the loss of credibility with their congregants. The FLDS Church fostered a culture that it was our duty to inform on others, and we lived lives in constant fear of being reported and vigilantly watched for other members to step out of line. Children were even encouraged to report on their parents. It felt like there were eyes all around you.

My dad and I had consistent run-ins over his not staying in line with the teachings of the FLDS Church. Sometimes as a kid and a teenager I challenged my dad over his lack of following the rules of the church, because I believed that we had to always obey the church in order to make it to heaven. There was a culture inside the FLDS Church of parents turning on their kids and kids turning on their parents. I personally called my dad out all of the time for doing things that were not in line with the teachings of the prophet. I wanted to do right by God. We all did, even if that meant betraying a parent or a child to serve Him.

Every Saturday priesthood holders (male heads of a household) and their sons were required to show up at a predetermined location to help other members fix or build things. It was always manual labor, a fence to build or a field to clear. Initially the requests were to come and volunteer. The word "volunteer" implied that you had a choice, although it was clearly a requirement. If you didn't show up, you'd be looked down on by the community. Sometimes my dad went, sometimes he didn't. Once he stopped going for several months and was called before one of the leaders of the church who told him it was mandatory that he and his boys went to help with Saturday work to avoid "big trouble". After that reprimand, my father would go help every Saturday and only rarely took the day off. I was in my early teens and completely supported the church. When he didn't go, I would become judgmental of my own father and would take him to task for it. The FLDS Church had such control over me that I was more loyal to the cult than my own father.

Seemingly little infractions like this were the kind of thing that would cause someone to lose their family. If the church came out with a new commandment and a man outright refused to obey it, the man's children and wives would be reassigned to another man. If you didn't openly refuse but more subtly slacked off like my dad did, after a time you'd also lose your family. Everyone knew this, everyone saw this happen to others.

PREACHING THE PRACTICE

Every time there was something coming up where they knew they'd be asking for something from the faithful, the sermons leading up would focus on obedience. There would be Bible and Book of Mormon stories about following the will of God and listening to the prophets for two or three weeks prior to the unveiling of the new commandment. Then after weeks of indoctrination, there would be a "test of our obedience" in the form of an added financial pressure or a new living restriction that we must now adhere to. There was nothing coincidental about the way these things were done, it was all deliberate. Obedience was framed as a test from God. Give your money, give your time, even sacrificing one's own family to demonstrate your faith and meet the needs of the church.

The people running the FLDS Church weren't stupid; they knew exactly what they were doing and every move was calculated. Warren Jeffs believed he was a genius and convinced his followers to follow him because he was God's prophet. Now that I have some perspective, after several years out of the cult, I don't think Jeffs had superior intellect but he was a very cunning and skilled manipulator.

The members of the FLDS Church aren't stupid, by any means. Whether they were raised in the faith or join as adults, they are intelligent individuals. Making decisions and navigating life, especially for people who have been indoctrinated since childhood, is hard. Giving away control of some of life's most difficult decisions to a trusted religious leader is comforting in many ways, and can make you feel safe. It is true this meant giving away your power to the group, but it also removed the responsibility for decisions. I never worried about whether or not I was doing the right things in my life because an authority figure I believed spoke for God was telling me exactly what to do. It wasn't until I left that I realized the cult was taking much more than they were giving. I don't blame the people for blindly following and obeying, I lay the responsibility at the feet of the leaders who took advantage of individual's fear and faith for their own personal benefit. Cults like the FLDS Church prey on human insecurities. Even intelligent, capable people can become victims if life throws the right obstacles in their paths. This is even truer if your parents were raised in the cult and it's the only thing you've ever known.

The level of fear is extreme; you're not just fearful about what will happen to you in this life, but for the salvation of your eternal soul.

Preaching from the pulpit was hell fire and damnation; the eternal consequences of making mistakes in this life and the effects on your children if you weren't living the right way were terrifying. The prophet and leaders made us believe we were at war fighting for our everlasting existence. They kept the stakes high at all times, in every situation, even for little children, so we were all fearful of making a wrong move and being tortured for eternity in hell.

WHO'S IN CONTROL?

A central theme to everyone's journey through life is control. It's tied to how we think of ourselves and how others think of us. It's a tight-rope, the balance between having control and letting someone else take the reins. At the beginning of life, we trust our parents who have control over us to use their power in the right way. A new baby can't be in control of their world, it's impossible. They have to depend on their parents for everything, from food, to bathing, to supporting their little heads. With every passing day, the growing baby gains more and more independence. It starts with a child holding up their own head, then reaching for things, then sitting up, crawling and finally walking on their own. These milestones are magical for parents but require a re-linquishing of control. Parents must determine when it is safe to allow a child to strike out on their own and even though it's painful, must allow them to fail and learn from their own mistakes. Children can gravitate to unhealthy authority figures if parents cut the apron strings too early. As a parent I believe obedience has a place, but the FLDS Church took their control too far. My opinion is, the line should be what's in the best interest of the child or adult. If the goal is to further your own self-interest or make yourself feel more powerful through control of another person, the control is wrong. Control should always be a temporary thing; a ladder to help people grow, not a cage.

When my dad was younger, in his mid-twenties, the FLDS Church's control and demands for obedience weren't as extreme. Every year it got a little worse, and with every new prophet the scope of control expanded. I remember principal Warren Jeffs implementing controls on students when I was in school that he later extended to the entire church membership when he became the prophet. He had been masterminding this control for a long time. In the FLDS Church membership it was well know that when Jeffs was younger he'd been obsessed with Hitler and other dictators, always reading about them. I believe Jeffs learned a lot about propaganda from these evil men and then used their tactics to control his FLDS followers. Looking back, I can clearly see how we were living under the same kind of controls that created extreme Nazi Germany and communist Russia.

The FLDS Church was very political; people did things to gain approval from the prophet and church leaders. The only reason my father was allowed to return to the church with a "gentile" (our word for an outsider) wife was because his Grandfather was a prominent member of the church. Your name meant everything; there was no way for a man to rise up from nothing. People did not leave the faith and then come back, so there was no "welcome home" for my father when he returned to the FLDS Church. It was more of a favor, and one the church leaders at the time didn't want to do, but felt obligated to do because of his Grandfathers name. Incidentally, all of my father's family have left the FLDS Church now. He had twelve or thirteen brothers and seven or eight sisters. Of those, one brother and three sisters came from my father's same mother; in polygamy it's hard to keep track of everyone.

Some of the most controversial aspects of the FLDS were evident in my family. My dad's sister was married to an old man when she was only twelve years old. She had two children with him. By the time

I was growing up in the church, thanks to the raid that occurred in the fifties, children were supposed to be eighteen to get married, but that wasn't a hard and fast rule. My father had a niece who married a man that I worked for when I was a teenager. She was thirteen and he was old enough to be her father. The man already had two wives. He was caught, prosecuted by the state, and sent to jail. It was the first time someone in the church had been prosecuted for statutory rape in many years and it scared everyone in the FLDS community. There were other child bride cases that the local authorities never prosecuted. It's important to understand that these men didn't choose girls to marry, Warren or Rulon Jeffs commanded older men to marry underage girls. The tradition of blind obedience was strong in the church and the cloak of silence deafening. I had a relative who married three underage girls and ended up in prison for twenty-five years. These men made the choice to go along with the prophet's orders, and they chose to start having children with underage girls who were just children themselves, but it's important to understand followers honestly believed the threat for their disobedience was eternal damnation.

I don't think the practice of plural marriages would have caused the local authorities to make arrests, if the practice hadn't involved minors, which constituted child abuse. Adults can choose to live alternative lifestyles, but when the FLDS Church started to command old men to marry and start having children with twelve-year-old girls, a line was crossed. This practice will never be accepted, nor should it. In the end, this is what landed Warren Jeffs on the FBI's Most Wanted List, right under Osama Bin Laden.

What outside authorities shaped your life?

How do you see authority in your life today?

What does control mean to you?

CHAPTER 7
MOMMY AND DADDY ISSUES

To share your weakness is to make yourself vulnerable.
To make yourself vulnerable is to show strength.
- Crissi Jami

That girl has daddy issues. That guy is a mama's boy. It's unfair to blame your mom and dad for everything that's gone wrong in your adult life, primarily because deflecting blame won't help you fix anything in the present. Gaining insight into how you got to be the way you are will give you a chance to change your life. I've come to realize my skewed views on religion, God, my parents and my family in general can be traced back to my upbringing in the FLDS Church.

FATHER AND MOTHER

"Hello father."

When I was in public or around other people in our church, I was only allowed to call my dad "father". It was a strict rule, like the other strict rules in the FLDS Church. My siblings and I made fun of it, laughing at the other kids, even though we had to do it ourselves.

My mom was always addressed as "mother" in public. Her sister, my dad's second wife, was addressed as "Mother Donna".

Men went by their last names, Uncle Doyle or Brother Dockstader. Women went by their first names. It gives me flashbacks when I start to go back over it all. In school, all of the prophet's wives taught classes and were also called by their first names, Mother Ora or Mother Loretta. One of my teachers and wife of the prophet, was just a few years older than I was. I had a crush on her, like any normal fifteen-year-old boy, because she was one woman I was allowed to talk to. In the FLDS Church the only girls I was allowed to speak to were my mothers, sisters, and my teachers. If a boy was caught speaking more than a word or two with a girl his age, he would be reprimanded by the church leaders.

This is an instance where the FLDS did a great job coding their members. It began with something as simple as having everyone call each other family names like "uncle" and "sister". This made us all feel like we were one, big family, and everyone knows families stick together. Regarding the separation of boys and girls, it seemed reasonable to prevent teenage boys and girls from spending time alone together. Most parents would agree that there's a point where kids that age need parental supervision. The rules slowly got more restrictive and the church's control more intrusive until girls and boys weren't even allowed to speak to each other.

Romantic relationships are a big part of our lives. People write songs and stories about love, we're obsessed with it. Love stories have inspired men and women throughout history dating all the way back to Adam and Eve. By controlling romantic relationships, the FLDS Church had a hell of a lot of control over people. They controlled their adult members and exercised control over the next generation through their children. That's power.

LACK OF ATTENTION, NOT LACK OF PRESENCE

I attribute my problems growing up to my parent's lack of attention towards me. They were always around, they never left me, but they spent so much of their time serving the church, working and raising their nine kids, there never seemed to be enough time to give each child the one-on-one attention needed.

This took me a long time to understand. I never thought of myself as a guy who had mommy and daddy issues until I was much older. My mom was home a lot and my dad worked hard to support us. Compared to the horrible things that kids outside my religion had to deal with, like parents who were on drugs or absent fathers, what did I have to complain about? Even in my religion, there were kids whose dads had ten wives and forty kids. How could I complain about my dad who just had two wives and ten kids neglecting me?

As a child, you believe your reality is normal, good and healthy. You think this is the way things should be, because it's all you know. As time passed, my views changed and I now believe there's a point when you have too many kids to adequately care for and it becomes child abuse. This doesn't just happen in large families, a single parent raising one or two kids can also fail to give them enough attention. Independence is good for children, but neglect is not. Being crammed in a house with so many people there was no way to get any type of one-on-one time, which was tough for me as a child, I felt pushed aside. I remember being told to go play with my siblings so we made up our own rules and tried to figure out life on our own with limited parental guidance. I don't feel like I formed any real relationships in my childhood.

As a parent, I think about my past a lot. I have to keep myself from focusing too much on how I'm unintentionally shaping my son. When my boy was younger, I worried about the subtlest little things because

I didn't want to be creating major personality hang-ups for him to deal with later in life. You can try to do everything right, but you'll inevitably screw up some parts of your child when you're parenting. My parents did their best with what they had, and I feel like I still have a lot of scars. I look at other people that I grew up with and see they had it so much worse and I feel fortunate to have had the parents I had.

At times I catch myself sounding like my own father. It's inherent, buried within me so that it comes out when I least expect it. My father was an emotionless man, like a lot of men and like all of the men in the FLDS Church. Phrases I remember him saying include "no crying", "don't be a wimp", "walk it off", "don't be a baby". I do believe that as a man it's important to be resilient. You need enough internal toughness to handle what the world will throw at you, and the world is designed to break men's spirits. That's another thing that I'm careful about now that I can see how the FLDS Church took this principle to an extreme level. I don't know that I would have survived the faith if my dad hadn't modeled toughness for me my whole life. My dad never complained, never cried, and never whined about anything. He was the most level, stoic, human being I've ever met. I think it was his survival tactic too.

My mom was the exact opposite. In our religion, where men were expected to be in complete control over their emotions at all times, women were allowed to be more emotional. My mom did push back and spoke her mind; she gave her opinion about anything and everything, the opposite of most of the women in the FLDS Church. She was one of the few women who did work, because some did have to leave the home. If they had kids at home, they'd have a sister wife keep them. Women who worked in the FLDS Church were limited in their choice of occupations usually cleaning houses or helping on farms. My mom cut hair because that's was her profession before she joined the FLDS Church. This was unusual because women weren't allowed to attend school outside of the FLDS community and female church members weren't permitted to cut their hair so a woman cutting another woman's hair was unheard of. I was cared for by Donna from the age of two until I went to school. Donna wasn't a kind woman or a loving parent to me and she didn't keep house well. Growing up I felt lucky to have my mom home with me for those first two years, but with so many siblings there was no such thing as one-on-one time with either parent. We had bedrooms with a couple sets of bunk beds in each room living tighter than kids in a college dorm. The FLDS Church's policy of distance between men and women also had a significant impact on my ability to sustain relationships as an adult. I simply didn't know how to do it.

One of my fondest childhood memories was being in the hospital with appendicitis when I was about nine. My mom and dad both came and spent time with me. No brothers or sisters, just me and them. I can't help but smile when I think about it and to this day, I love hospitals because of this experience. I remember my parents brought pizza into the room when I could finally eat, and even Warren Jeffs visited me and prayed over me. It's odd to think of him sitting in a jail cell now because back then I saw him as a holy man.

Creating a home where kids have parent involvement but also learn independence is a delicate balance. It's something that I'm working on with my own son, and only time will tell if my strategy worked for him.

FATHER'S DAY, MOTHER'S DAY

Every year on Father's Day and Mother's Day, my social media is full of people from my old life posting pictures of their parents.

"This is my dad, I haven't seen him in fifteen years."

"Here's my mom, we haven't spoken since I was seventeen."

It's one of the heartbreaking results of leaving the FLDS Church. There is no halfway in the church, you're either in or out. If you're in, you're subject to all of the strict edicts that go on inside. If you're out, the church teaches you lose your eternal soul, and your family too. People get kicked out for talking to people who have left and it's considered a sin to have communication with family members who are outside of the FLDS Church. It's believed that they've fallen into sin and can't be saved. Once you go, you must stay gone. There's no repentance, there's no turning back, there's no salvation.

Not everyone leaves by choice, a lot are kicked out against their will. Usually it's the men who get kicked out, women are rarely asked to leave. The primary reason for this is that women and children are considered currency in the FLDS Church. The church only works if there are a lot more women than men in it, allowing male church members to have multiple wives. It's also typically the men that apostatize from the church, not women. I remember one woman who left a very prominent man in the church and faced a massive court battle to try and secure custody of their kids. Women in the FLDS Church have no marketable skills and no access to money, so it is very hard for them to leave.

So what happens to the extra guys? A lot of them die in construction accidents; I went to many funerals during my teen years of men who had been killed while on the job. A lot of men leave because they have some contact with the outside world and decide they don't want to live within the strict confines of the church. That's why I left. Finally, there are the men who were kicked out of the church as punishment for some sin, often they aren't even told what the sin was. Their wives (remember only the first marriage is legal) are assigned to another man, raising that man's status in the FLDS community. Boys and men who have left or been kicked out of the FLDS Church are ostracized by their families. Would you risk your eternal soul to talk to your son who had sinned? A common "sin" that did get women kicked out of the FLDS community was talking to their children who weren't in the church anymore.

SEED BEARERS

I spent a lot of time in school until the ninth grade when the FLDS School closed its doors and I went to work. We didn't learn any world history, but we were taught a lot about "priesthood history" or the fathers of the church and were required to memorize the prophets all the way back to Adam in the Bible.

The power of this kind of coding is undeniable. Everything in the world I grew up in was shaped through the lens of the FLDS Church by the church leaders. This control became more intense every year, slowly progressing until the prophet could convince people to do things that they'd otherwise never dream of doing. You can condition someone to do anything if you code them well. The good news is utilizing these same principles, you can get yourself anywhere you want to go, once you learn to code yourself in the right direction.

The Church demanded respect from its followers but didn't earn it. Children were taught to treat all adults with great respect, almost like every man was a holy man. There were egos everywhere, all based on status. Like a pack of wolves, the alpha male was in charge of the church. I remember huge Fourth of July gatherings with my grandmother's family, the Steeds. They were a very prominent family in the FLDS community and owned a huge compound in Salt Lake City with over thirty thousand square feet surrounded by a ten foot wall. We were all Steeds through marriage, so hundreds of people gathered for the event annually. One of the men, Truman Barlow, was a prominent figure in the Church. He'd been First Counselor to Leroy Johnson, the Prophet before Rulon Jeffs, and then First Counselor to Rulon. I remember one Fourth of July celebration when Truman Barlow was paraded through hundreds of people with all of his sons, grown men, following him. It felt like the President of the United States was in the crowd. I was a little kid pulling on people's pants legs asking "Who's that?" with wide eyes. I didn't know who he was, but realized he must be someone really important. "That's Uncle Truman," someone explained. He had five or six wives and thirty or forty kids, a man of incredible status in the FLDS Church revered by the community.

The more prominent the man, the more wives he had. Imagine having twenty or thirty siblings and five women living in the same house. A man with five wives basically walked on water, unless he stepped out of line. Then he'd lose it all and become just some old guy with nothing to show for his life. Women had no power or say in who they were assigned to. They were passed around from man to man with no choice in the matter. Men also didn't get to choose their wives, but at least they could climb the social ladder.

When a boy became a man, he could go to the leadership of the Church and ask for a piece of land. Then he'd built a house on it and hope to be given a wife to start his adult life. From there, he could eventually get more wives and more children, more currency to grow his prominence in the church. Some of it was determined by your bloodline, names carried a lot of weight in the FLDS Church, but then everyone was related so more depended on your status or popularity with the current church leaders. My dad's brother built a house on church land and grew his family, then was kicked out of the Church for some misdeed and lost everything. When the state intervened ten years ago he was able to prove he built the house and it was returned to him. Not every man was so lucky. My dad followed my mom out of the FLDS Church keeping our family together until he died.

The FLDS Church believes in eternal life and eternal bonds. The Mormon Church is the same with their weddings in the Temple. If you get your wedding sealed, then you and your wife are bound together for eternity. Your children are bound together with you too. The difference is that in the FLDS Church, the prophet can break or dissolve those eternal bonds. The FLDS believe the prophet is the voice of God on earth, and this doctrine became more intense with each new prophet. Warren married several of his dad's wives after Rulon died. Polygamy seems strange to outsiders whose only form of reference is a reality TV show, but for those who had grown up in the culture it didn't seem unusual. The doctrine said a man in the FLDS Church had to have at least three wives to get into the highest level in heaven. Once a man had five wives, nine didn't seem so crazy. If nine was ok then fifteen was too. Suddenly the prophet had forty wives and the ages of those wives kept creeping down until he was marrying young girls.

The FLDS Church could never have enforced extreme practices like allowing another man to have sex with your wife while you watched without slow, gradual changes over time. Reports made available through the courts to the public exposed a culture in the FLDS Church where only certain men who were deemed worthy in the eyes of the church were allowed to have sex with women and father children. Husbands were forced to stay in the room holding the hands of their wives while they were raped by one or even multiple men in succession. It is my understanding that if a man in the FLDS Church even holds hands with his wife now they could both be kicked out. In the FLDS Church we were told again and again that everyone was free to exercise their free agency and leave the church at any time. It didn't feel like a truly free choice when the cost of leaving was losing your family, home and your eternal soul.

Where did adult attention come from in your childhood?

Describe your relationship with your parents. How does it influence you today?

ONLY THOSE
WHO RISK GOING
TOO FAR, CAN
POSSIBLY FIND
OUT HOW FAR
ONE CAN GO.

—ERIC THOMAS

CHAPTER 8
RULES

Strong minds discuss ideas.
Average minds discuss events.
Weak minds discuss people.
- Socrates

The rules that we had to follow as members of the FLDS Church covered every aspect of life from what we had to wear, to how we could spend our money, to our interactions with our spouses in the bedroom. There were always new rules being added as edicts from the church as the church leadership expanded their control over their followers. We didn't always know what the consequences of breaking the rules would be. It could be something as simple as a stern reprimand or as major as losing your family. The target moved constantly, and at the end of the day we were all at the mercy of the leaders of the church.

RULES ABOUT OUTSIDE CONTACT

Everything in the FLDS Church was designed to limit our contact with the outside world and instead focus on the prophet who was preparing an army of people for the end of the world. We were taught that the world beyond our walls was evil. Just coming into contact with it put us at risk of being poisoned by it, like a disease. We were told someone wouldn't even know they had contracted this outside influence until it was too late, and we'd potentially infect the people we love. We feared the outside world the way people fear plagues, nuclear bombs or terrorist attacks. This isolation was a powerful form of control for the FLDS Church and included:

- No television
- No radio
- No secular music
- No movies
- No public school
- No public places, like bars or concerts
- No alcohol
- No reading of non-approved books
- No talking to people not in the FLDS Church more than absolutely necessary
- Don't tell people which church you belong to
- Don't evangelize or try to recruit
- No talking to people who have left the church or have been kicked out
- Polygamy is illegal, keep it a secret

Unlike most mainstream religions, the FLDS Church doesn't proselytize. We didn't want outsiders to come in, the idea was to grow the church by members having more kids. It was taught that outside people would taint the bloodline that went back to Adam. We were God's chosen people, the pure race.

This extended to extreme racism in the FLDS Church. We were taught white people were superior and similar fallacies were discussed often. The FLDS teaches that before the world began, Jesus and Satan were at war in heaven. Satan said "Let's make everyone on Earth be obedient to God's commandments and they'll be saved and everyone will be permitted into heaven." Jesus disagreed, saying, "People need to have the freedom to make their own choices, and that will lead them to either heaven or hell." This argument between God's two sons went on and on, with some angels taking Jesus's side and other angels taking Satan's side. According to scripture, the angels who chose to follow Satan were cast into hell with him and became demons. The FLDS Church teaches not everyone in heaven took sides during the war and those who were on the fence were cursed with dark skin. Today, I find this teaching deeply offensive and can't imagine how anyone believes it.

Despite the FLDS Church's strict rules, my dad would sometimes take us to movies. I remember seeing Jurassic Park in a theater and when I returned to school after, I knew which of my friends I could tell and who the little snitches were. I shared every detail of the movie while the boys sat with their eyes big, listening intently. As I grew up I too became more extreme. I remember later when I was seventeen and working construction snow hindered our work one day and we had an afternoon to ourselves. I was self-righteous and determined to follow the teachings of the church so when one guy suggested that we go to a movie, I put a stop to it and prevented myself and the rest of the group of young men from breaking the church rules.

Not everyone followed the rules perfectly, in fact, part of the culture of secrecy was hiding from the church leadership when you broke the rules. Technically alcohol consumption was prohibited, but lots of church members drank. I had friends, nephews of the prophet, who drank beer and for years it was an open secret. When I was fourteen, I was out working and got a ride home with one of my friends. He was married to one of Rulon Jeff's daughters and she rode along in the car with us. When we pulled up to my house you could see the blue glow of a screen through the blinds of a bedroom. Immediately she said "Aha!" and questioned me about it, sure she'd caught us breaking the no TV rule. This was a daughter of the prophet with a reputation for being a tattletale and this type of an infraction could get someone kicked out of the church. We did have a TV, but that particular glow was a computer screen and fortunately members were allowed to have computers for work so I explained it was a computer, not a TV. At that time in my life I was working to be devout and if it had been the TV I honestly don't know if I could have lied to protect my family.

The FLDS community was dependent on the outside world for money. My dad worked for a printing business outside the FLDS community in Colorado City, Arizona. He wasn't allowed to talk about his religion or to have anything but strict business relationships with his coworkers. No company softball games or Christmas parties, the edict was to avoid interacting unless conducting business.

We were also dependent on the outside world for healthcare. We didn't believe that science or medicine was a bad thing if it helped us, so there were many instances of FLDS church members receiving medical treatment at the local hospital. The Prophet Rulon Jeffs spent a lot of time in the hospital near the end of his life. The exception was births in the FLDS community. Births to underage mothers and plural wives had to be kept a secret because they were illegal. Mother Sharon, one of Rulon's wives, was a midwife and many women in the FLDS church were nurses. They birthed hundreds of babies in a special wing of the prophet's house set up with all kinds of medical equipment for that purpose. A woman would go into labor and have the baby, then stay for a couple of days to recuperate, just like in secular hospitals. I was one of those babies, born in the prophet's house. There were church records kept but it was common for children not to have state-issued birth certificates until they were older and needed them. I remember a seventeen-year-old teacher saying she needed to go get her birth certificate before she could secure her driver's license. Outside of the FLDS Church, no one knew she existed.

RULES ABOUT SEX, MARRIAGE, AND HOME

The rules about sex and marriage in the FLDS Church were probably the most controlling because they were more intimate than other commandments. For most of society, adults get to decide what happens in the bedroom, it's private. Rules in the FLDS Church included:

- No dating
- No flirting
- No contact with members of the opposite sex
- Marriage partners are assigned
- No dancing
- Wedding ceremonies are simple
- No sex except for procreation purposes
- No showing of affection, not even between parents and children
- No hard and fast rule for the age of marriage
- No trinkets
- No false idols
- Utilitarian home

Physical contact of any kind including hugging is taboo in the FLDS Church. In the later years even holding hands between a husband and wife could be considered a sin. Anything could be deemed crossing the line, members were always watching each other. There was constant gossip because even though we couldn't participate in a certain behavior we could talk about other people sinning freely.

We had co-ed education in school but it was almost like the girls weren't there. You could say a pleasantry like hello, but that was all that was allowed. That didn't keep us from thinking about women, though. My friends and I would imagine passionate love affairs from simply making eye contact with a girl. When we were older we'd drive by a girl's house, sometimes over and over, just to catch a glimpse of our crush if she stepped outside for a few minutes. It was admittedly weird, I know that now, but in the FLDS community it seemed normal. We all knew that if we worked hard enough and were granted a marriage, it would not be to a woman we chose, it would be the prophet's choice.

Marriages were simple and often a surprise. I knew guys who just got a phone call out of nowhere saying "you're going to get married tomorrow morning," that was typical. They'd go put on their Sunday clothes and head out to the prophet's house where the ceremony was performed. When my sister was married, the wedding ceremony lasted for thirty minutes and the potluck dinner for a couple of hours. I remember talking to Warren Jeffs at his house where the wedding was performed after the ceremony. The bride would then move in with her new husband and that was the end of the recognition, no honeymoon or fanfare.

Sex for pleasure, even inside of marriage, was cause for excommunication. It could only be used for procreation. If a husband and wife had sex after they knew she was pregnant, that would be grounds to be kicked out of the church. Especially for men, women were rarely kicked out to avoid shortages of wives within the community. Men were expendable, seen as competition. They'd kick out forty-nine men so that one of the leaders could have fifty wives. Warren Jeffs saw the growing imbalance and started kicking more young men out of the FLDS community; the news media called them the "Lost Boys".

Back in the early days of US History girls often married young as soon as they reached puberty and this trend continued into the early 1800's. Over time, norms changed, and many states set their legal marrying age at 18, but even today there are 13 states in the US with no legal marrying age. In Utah, the current legal age for marriage is 18 but 16 year olds can marry with the consent of their parents or guardians and 15 year old's can marry with court approval. After the FLDS Church was busted in the fifties for performing underage marriages, the FLDS Church enforced a strict marrying age of eighteen for a long time. Later the restriction was lessened to allow girls to marry at seventeen, as long as the father decided it as ok. Under Warren Jeffs' leadership the age for girls was dropped to fifteen and then down to twelve. Men almost always had to be eighteen to marry because of the hierarchy.

FLDS member's homes had to be as plain and utilitarian as possible, beautifications were frowned upon. The prophet would walk into someone's house and tell them to take things off the walls if he thought it was too pompous. All homes had huge living and dining rooms to accommodate large families. No televisions or entertainment systems were allowed, just couches lining the walls and huge dining room tables. Kitchens were massive with industrial equipment for cooking for dozens of people.

Everything around marriage, family, and the home centered on making children and following the prophet, giving him extraordinary power.

RULES ABOUT CLOTHING

Beyond the rules on home and family, the FLDS controlled clothing very closely. It's a form of self-expression, and stopping that form of agency went a long way to prohibit people from thinking for themselves. The FLDS Church leaders never wanted their members to feel empowered or in control. Dressing the wrong way was serious and if it happened consistently you could get into really big trouble. The rules about clothing and appearance were strictly enforced and included:

- Wearing red is strictly forbidden
- Plain fabrics, no bold patterns or colors
- Clothing from wrist to ankle for both men and women
- Long underwear beneath clothing, also wrist to ankle
- Women only wear dresses, never pants
- Women cannot cut their hair, and must always wear it up
- Men have short hair, but not too short
- No facial hair
- No makeup
- No piercings
- No bracelets
- No crosses
- No adornments of any kind

Red was forbidden because it's the color that Jesus is prophesied to wear when he comes back to the earth for the rapture. Red wasn't allowed anywhere in our lives, not on our clothes or in our houses. Even red cars were forbidden. In August, 2006 when Warren Jeffs was arrested in Vegas he was wearing shorts, a t-shirt, and riding in a red vehicle. His favorite wife, Naomi, was with him wearing jeans and a short sleeve bright pink shirt with her hair down.

Anything that was meant to enhance your appearance was an affront to God in the FLDS Church. We were told that the clothing rules were to keep our bodies as temples to God and to prevent sexual desire. We had to be covered up at all times, in every situation. When I was about six years old, before Warren Jeffs took over, his father the prophet Rulon Jeffs rented out a water park so all FLDS Church members could go swimming and enjoy the water slides in a private party setting. We swam fully clothed, in long sleeved shirts and pants with our long underwear worn underneath, the girls in long skirts. It was one of the most fun excursions we had, though looking back it was probably pretty dangerous because our clothes got heavy when wet, adding twenty pounds and causing us to sink to the bottom of the pool. As a child I was oblivious to the dangers, I didn't care, it was just fun.

The clothing was normal for us within the FLDS community but people not of our faith would stare at us, point and whisper when we went out in public to the store. Not so much for the boys, but definitely for the girls. The boys looked pretty normal, just a little dressed up in our buttoned shirts and jeans, but whenever my mom or sisters were with me in public, I felt ashamed because they were dressed so differently from secular women and girls.

RULES ABOUT MONEY

Women and children were a major form of "currency" in the FLDS Church. The number of wives and children a man had was more an indicator of his place in heaven than his financial status in this life. Initially it sounds good that followers didn't measure status by how much money one had, but determining a man's hierarchy by number of wives and children was a whole lot worse.

The FLDS Church leadership did worry about lining their pockets. Members were encouraged to make as much money as possible to give back to the church in the form of donations, some illegal, including:

- Ten percent tithe is required from all families
- Give extra money to the Church when asked
- Donate labor to the Church when asked
- State monies are turned over to the Church
- Real estate is put into the Church's name

However you boil it down, the FLDS Church is a business. They held a trust of ten million dollars, with a lot more squirreled away and held in real estate properties. The propaganda that members were always told was that the FLDS Church was broke, but that was far from true. Warren Jeffs, his brother, and his father Rulon were all accountants, they knew exactly what they were doing. Running the church as a non-profit organization meant they were exempt from paying taxes.

FLDS Church members donated unquestioningly. We didn't realize we were being exploited to put money into the pocket of the FLDS leaders. I remember having to chase my paychecks when I worked for companies associated with the FLDS. Unlike a normal company where you work and get your check on a set date, in the FLDS you'd go to your boss and ask for a paycheck and they'd ask you why you needed it. I remember making the case that my family needed the money, but that didn't always mean I'd get paid. This was in addition to all of the free work we did for the FLDS Church on the weekends. Men would keep sending money to the church, even after they were excommunicated because they believed their eternal souls were at stake.

FLDS-owned companies fed their profits into a central bank account. Women were part of the money-making scheme too, they'd tell FLDS women to go get food stamps from the state and then bring the cards back to the church officials. The food would then be bought and put into a central storehouse, instead of being distributed to the underfed kids in the community. Lyle Jeffs, Warren Jeff's brother, went to prison for his involvement in this type of fraud.

Fraud was everywhere. Though we were outwardly godly people, we were never allowed to be honest in the FLDS Church. Lying to the government about taxes, real estate, and government support programs were just ways we manipulated the secular world. We believed Warren Jeffs was our prophet and president and we didn't recognize or answer to the false US government. Everyone outside the FLDS Church was perceived as evil. That meant you could lie to them or cheat them and it wasn't considered a sin.

RULES ABOUT FAITH

Warren Jeffs would often say: "Pray always, always be praying." That was the commandment; we were directed to constantly be praying and talking to God. As long as God told you things that fell in line with the church's teachings, you were right to obey, but if you started to receive personal revelation that didn't gel with what Warren or Rulon Jeffs said, you were told that wasn't God talking to you, it was the devil in your ear. Here are the FLDS Church's rules on prayer and religious observances:

- Pray twice a day with the family
- Pray before meals
- Church on Sunday
- Third Saturday night of the month men go to the Priesthood meeting
- Religion is incorporated into school, homeschool, or an FLDS school

- FLDS history is world history
- The Prophet is the final word on everything

We were taught religion had the answers to everything. Any question that you had or anything that happened in your life could be explained through FLDS teachings.

Men were required to attend priesthood meetings once a month. This was how you progressed in the FLDS Church. Similar to the Church of Jesus Christ of Latter-day Saints' priesthood structure where men advance from deacon to teacher to priest in the Aaronic Priesthood, which dates back to Aaron in the Bible. In the higher or Melchizedek Priesthood men advanced from elders to high priests. Similarly in the FLDS Church on Saturday nights we'd participate by going through the priesthood levels. At twelve you were a deacon, fourteen a teacher, sixteen a priest, and at eighteen a Melchizedek priest. The further you got, the more power you had. Starting out at twelve as a deacon I felt like I was someone, like I had value. There was nothing similar for the girls.

Despite my religious upbringing, I never felt as connected to God as I wanted to be. Spirituality was rules and regulations, less about doing good than not being bad. After all that I experienced, even today, I can still see good in some of the FLDS Church's teachings. Not everything that I learned as a child was bad. Some of the things the Church forbid me to do, I've chosen to continue not doing on my own after leaving the church. Some of the stuff that I was forbidden to do, I now embrace. The important difference is that now I make decisions on my own. I understand the coding I experienced in my childhood came from a cult, not God, and I have the power to re-code myself as an adult moving forward.

Were there strict rules or a lack of rules in your formative years? Reflect on how this affected you.

Would you describe yourself as a rule follower or a rule breaker?

What rules do you think are important in your life today?

IT IS TIME TO UNLEARN THE THINGS YOU LEARNED FROM WOUNDED PEOPLE

CHAPTER 9
SOMETIMES THE
GRASS IS GREENER

Yesterday I was clever, so I wanted to change the world.
Today I am wise, so I am changing myself.

- Rumi

You cannot escape the past, but sometimes the grass really is greener on the other side.

I was eighteen when I decided to leave the FLDS Church. It was the impulsive decision of a young man who didn't know a damn thing about the world, but did realize that my future wasn't inside the walls that Warren Jeffs put up. Whether it was going to damn me to hell or not, I decided that I didn't care. At the time, the FLDS community believed the rapture was near and the apocalypse could happen at any moment. I didn't think I'd make it to heaven either way, so I determined I would rather go out and enjoy the time I had left before I was damned to hell.

I'd been thinking about leaving the church for a long time. I left home when I was fourteen and the FLDS high school closed. At the time I had the choice to be homeschooled or to start working, I chose work. There were injuries along the way, sometimes severe. When I got hurt, my boss would just shift me to a job that wasn't as demanding. It was illegal for kids my age to be working full-time, especially construction jobs. One positive thing about working in the building industry was that I was able to travel all over Colorado and Utah and see places that I never would have seen otherwise. On the road rooming with my buddies out of the confines of the FLDS Church we did have some freedoms simply because we weren't being watched all of the time. A lot of young men like me left the church around that same time.

It can take big choices for big changes to happen. There are pivotal events in everyone's life, times when we must all choose to create huge changes in our lives. Big decisions are necessary, but one mistake people make is thinking that simply making the choice is enough, Those leaps are just the beginning. You have to work hard to change your daily habits and your life. That's a lesson that took me more than a decade to learn.

TAKE THE LEAP

I was living at home in Salt Lake City in June 2001 when I finally made the leap and left the FLDS Church. My story is not as dramatic as many other people who left, but it was a huge, life-altering decision for me. A good friend of mine had just left four or five months earlier and he called me up and asked if I wanted to go out with him. I said sure, because my dad was out of town. He told me that we'd be going to a club and the FLDS clothes just weren't going to cut it, so we went shopping. I remember that I had no idea what my individual style was so I picked the loudest colors and patterns possible. Most of the young people who left the FLDS Church dressed flashy like me at first, in protest of the bland, conservative clothes we'd been forced to wear as children. I can still recall the insane shirt with flames down the sleeves I picked out, I had no idea what was cool. This moment was a huge deal. I'd never worn anything but long underwear, jeans and plain, long-sleeve shirts. When I put on these "gentile clothes" I realized I couldn't turn back. I stood there looking in the mirror and I could feel that something had changed inside me and I wasn't a part of the FLDS community anymore. The simple act of changing my clothes changed my life. Long underwear, pants and long-sleeved shirts are uncomfortable so it's true, sometimes the grass really is greener.

The next day I sat down with my mom and told her. Her words were along the lines of, "Good for you, go for it." She never tried to stop me and I think she was excited to see her son explore the world. My dad begged me to stay, but he didn't stand in the way of me leaving. I wasn't the first member of my family to leave, I had an older brother who had left shortly before I did. My parents knew it was a possibility because I'd always been so headstrong. I created a new life for myself, but was very fortunate not to lose my family. My parents never stopped talking to me. My siblings never shunned me.

I had to quit my job because I was doing construction for an FLDS-owned company at the time and "apostates" who had left the church weren't permitted to work for the church. I moved into the house where my friend was living because there was a room for rent, and I started a new job with a construction company not affiliated with the FLDS. Living my life on the outside was exciting and terrifying.

ESCAPING MY CODING

The funny thing is that when I was faithful and obedient in the FLDS Church, I never felt good. I lived with the constant struggle to keep the commandments and obey all the rules, always unsure about whether I was going in the right direction and following the teachings exactly. It was a battle against my own thoughts and feelings that felt unwinnable. I believed that if I just worked harder and prayed more it would get easier, but it never did. I desperately wanted to be a good person and I was coded to think that a good person must be perfect.

Leaving was hard, not just because of the physical separation from my family, friends, and community, but because I really wanted to believe the church was true. I wanted heaven to be on the other side of death, waiting for me. There's a sureness in this type of group people gravitate to in a world of uncertainties. The outside world seems scarier and more menacing than the scary and menacing things the leaders inside the FLDS Church were doing. Despite all my reservations, I knew it was the right time for me to leave and that quiet internal confidence gave me the strength to take the leap into the unknown.

Leaving wasn't as simple as I hoped it would be. I thought once I was gone I could put it all behind me, but that's not how change works, my coding was too ingrained in every part of my life to just turn off. It turned out to be a lot like quitting alcohol or any other kind of addiction, there were relapses. I had to construct a whole new way of thinking in order to get myself out of old habits, and that didn't happen overnight.

In the FLDS Church I had been sheltered, almost like living on another planet, and I had no idea what to expect in the outside world. It was completely different and totally unknown to me. I worked construction with my buddy, and instead of earning five dollars an hour like the polygamists paid, I was now making nineteen dollars an hour. I never had to go beg for my paycheck, they just handed it to me. It was more money than I'd ever imagined, but I also didn't realize how expensive it was to support myself; that was a rude awakening. I realized how much I had depended on the resources of my family for my food, shelter, clothes, and transportation. Making my own money felt great, but also lonely for a young man with no world experience.

The only thing I can think of to compare it to is losing someone to death. My decision to leave the FLDS Church felt final because I was letting my old life die and I couldn't go back. The only reason my father was able to leave the church as a child and return as an adult was because his mother hadn't chosen to leave. In the fifties, when the police raided the FLDS community, her husband sent her and their children to New Mexico to avoid being prosecuted for polygamy and going to jail. Because of these unique circumstances, my dad was able to rejoin the FLDS Church as an adult, but our family was still considered different from other FLDS families. My whole world changed and a part of myself died when I left the FLDS Church. I'd made the decision to change it, but it would take more than a decade for me to unpack the impact of leaving on my life.

For years I just relied on my survival instincts and didn't stop to think how my adult life was affected by my childhood. I was on autopilot. I chose the wrong girls to fill my loneliness, friendships for ease, and jobs for money. I thought that if I could just find the right job or the perfect girl, all the problems in my life would just magically be fixed. Unfortunately, without rewriting my coding I was still looking for validation and leadership from people outside of myself.

The secret is you'll stay stuck in the same cycle until you realize that no one can improve your life, but you. You must change yourself. You'll repeat the mistakes of your past, the ones that are holding you back, again and again if you're blaming your decisions on other people. This cycle finally stopped for me, when I started taking responsibility for my actions and living with intention.

ESCAPING MY GUILT

Some of us have to hit rock bottom to figure out who we are. You don't get to a point where you want to kill yourself overnight. Suicide goes against our DNA, the fight or flight instincts that keep us safe and are hard-wired into each and every living creature. I put a gun in my mouth after years of downhill slide culminating in one moment of crisis. It's catastrophic, but not something that drops on you like a bomb. In the same way the FLDS Church leaders gradually led people through small steps to huge acts of wrongdoing, like raping children.

During my upbringing, I was never encouraged to think for myself or follow my own heart. Everything was dictated by the FLDS Church rules and the only thing that mattered was what church leaders said was right or wrong for us to do. If no one saw you do it, it was still a sin, so I internalized everything. I was taught whatever was wrong or sinful must have come from me, leading to a lot of guilt. I constantly felt inadequate and was convinced I was going to hell. The level of perfection that was pushed on us was impossible to live up to. The church leaders knew this, it was one of their many forms of manipulation. When things went wrong in my life after I left I felt like I shouldn't blame the FLDS Church for my problems. After all, my parents are good people and I was never physically or verbally abused.

When I walked away from the FLDS Church, I also left my moral compass behind. Suddenly, there was no guidance on where to go, no framework to understand the meaning and purpose of life. After years of being told what to do down to the smallest detail, no one was dictating how to dress or behave anymore or advising me on how to navigate women and vices. So I held to the guidance that I grew up with, in a piecemeal sort of way.

I was coded with certain thoughts and behaviors after years of living with the reality that I could be doing things wrong without even knowing it and held accountable for actions I didn't realize were wrong, like Warren Jeffs scolding me for my short hair. I was accustomed to being watched constantly and always worrying about what someone might see or say to me. I lived with constant feeling of guilt that weighed me down like the layers of wet clothes the day we all went swimming for the FLDS Church excursion when I was a kid.

Growing up I had also learned to rely on external validation and sought acceptance from other people because my parents were always busy with their other kids, work, or serving the Church. I craved attention and would often find it in unhealthy sources in the outside world. I married the first girl I dated because I still wanted to wait until marriage to have sex, but I was young and wanted to have sex. I still wanted to do the right things in my life, I just didn't want the FLDS Church dictating what was right for me.

I didn't understand any of this in the first years after I walked away from the FLDS Church, so It kept building and building inside of me until I found myself on my front lawn with the barrel of a gun in my mouth and my finger on the trigger. Not everyone has to hit rock bottom to decide to change their lives and recode themselves. The unaddressed issues inside of you are going to catch up with you and the sooner you address them the better your chance of avoiding rock bottom.

You cannot escape the past. Many people think that's the secret, but it's not. It's there with you everywhere you go and that's not necessarily a bad thing, if you can conquer the negative aspects associated with it, like guilt from things that happened in the past. This is the path to making your life what you want it to be and overcoming the negative coding of your own childhood experiences. The grass on the other side of dealing with your coding is greener.

What guilt are you carrying with you? Look at it from the outside and try to determine whether it's justified.

What parts of yourself do you feel you're trying to escape? You don't have to deal with them right now, just identify them.

Name three positive life changes that you've made as an adult

CHAPTER 10
SELF REVIEW

No man is free who is not the master of himself.

- Epictetus

What do you want and why do you want it? These are basic questions. So basic that we don't think to ask them. We switch to auto-pilot and go through the motions never understanding that we are making choices that affect the trajectory of our lives. From the moment we wake up we are faced with choices. You carry a mindset with you into every single day that affects the choices that you make. That mindset comes directly from the life experiences you've had to date. You can change it, but only if you're willing to put in the work.

You know who you are, even if you struggle to come to terms with that reality in your mind. I know that I'm terrible at being fake, I'm blunt and often speak before thinking and my insincerity is obvious and can offend people, so I often remain silent in social settings. Some people find this off-putting and think I'm rude, self-absorbed, or don't like them. The truth is that I don't naturally think about how my actions are making others feel, I really have to focus to be empathetic. I've always been my own person, and the center of my own experience. I think this is true for most people, whether they acknowledge it or not. It's not necessarily a bad thing because we need to secure our own physical and mental wellbeing first before we can help others.

I believe no one is more important in your life than you are. There's no shame in that, problems arise when we don't put the work and understanding into ourselves because we're so worried about other people that we neglect our own health. You have to fix yourself first.

When I left the FLDS religion I felt like I was faking a lot of interactions, trying to live the "right" way although I had no idea what was "right" anymore. I told myself I didn't care what anyone thought of me, it was all about me and what I wanted out of life. The problem is that I didn't know what I really wanted or what would bring me true happiness, even though I thought I did. I didn't have the tools to deal with the deep questions I was asking myself, so I escaped with alcohol and work. Drinking numbed my brain and senses and work kept me busy, but neither could completely suppress my desire to understand who I was. The questions never went away, but because I wasn't doing the work to answer them for myself, I lost sight of who I was becoming: a "tell it like it is", overly confident, and selfish person who destroyed relationships, and blamed everyone and everything but himself.

Over the last few years, that bluntness has become more subtle. I've done a lot of self-review and have figured out that coming down like a hammer doesn't always get me where I want to be. I feel like this change has improved my relationships with others and boosted my own self-esteem. All of this positive change started with honest self-review and introspection.

YOU DON'T KNOW WHAT YOU DON'T KNOW

If you want to know how to make changes in your life, you have to figure out where you are. Reviewing why you are the way you are is an important step in personal growth. When you know who you are, that's when you can take control of your life. Becoming self-aware will help you to see yourself in an accurate light. You don't know what you don't know about yourself unless you go looking for it. Even when you know yourself well, it's always going to be a process of re-evaluation.

I grew up in such a structured environment in the FLDS community where everything was laid out for me that I never had a chance to reflect on myself. Everything that defined me came from outside influences. You don't have to grow up in that same kind of strict environment to experience the same effects I did. It's common for people like parents, teachers and religious leaders to push their ideas of who you are or should become on you in your childhood. When we are young, most of us are unaware of these forces shaping us.

I had no idea what I didn't know or what forces were driving me forward when I started out on my journey of self-discovery. I was conflicted and thought the solution was to exchange one religion for another, so I joined the Church of Jesus Christ of Latter-day Saints, because it was the church the FLDS broke away from and many of the teachings were similar. I was still looking for religion to answer my questions about the purpose of life and to solve my problems. I had a deep appreciation for faith from my upbringing and wanted to keep that connection. I felt lost and looked to the rules of the Mormon Church to replace the rules of the FLDS Church in my life. It was a genuine search for me and I found aspects of healing and reconciliation during this time. Even with that, my early twenties were a time of recklessness where I looked everywhere for the keys to my happiness and never felt like I'd actually found them.

Once I made the huge decision to step away from the religion I'd known my whole life, I felt powerful. This reinforced my belief that

I'd made a good choice and was more knowledgeable than I really was. When you're young you tend to think that you have all of the answers, even though you don't have enough life experience to have really any. It's never a good idea to think you know it all, because no one does.

The alternative to growing is stagnating. All the years that I thought I was moving forward with my life because events were happening, money was made, and relationships were formed, I was actually sinking. It wasn't until I actively started to see opportunities for growth that my life started moving in the direction I wanted it to go.

PLANTING WEEDS IN YOUR OWN GARDEN

The person that you talk to the most is you. Everyone has an inner monologue, things that they say to themselves throughout the day. The way that self-talk plays out is important, and people get hung up on it.

When you talk through things negatively, you're planting weeds in your own garden. Think about it, you spend all of this time trying to do good things in your life. You put down roots with your job, with your relationships. You water your garden with education or vacation. You try to plant new things in your garden to make it better, like going to church or having children. With negative self-talk, you're undoing all of the hard work that you've put into yourself and filling that garden with weeds. Weeds don't just sit in our gardens inert, they grow bigger, spreading quickly, blocking out the sun, and soaking up the water and nutrients in the ground. This happens exponentially, until there's no room in your garden for the good things you've been planting and the weeds kill off the flowers, vegetables and fruits that you worked so hard to cultivate. It's counterintuitive and self-sabotage but people do it all the time, then can't figure out why they fail to reach the goals they set for themselves.

The first step is to stop planting weeds. This can be a hard habit to break if you've been doing it for a long time. Next you must kill the weeds if you're going to make any progress in taking back your garden.

My primary method of negative self-talk was related to guilt because it was a manipulation tool used on me by FLDS Church leaders during my formative years. This was one of the toughest parts of my coding for me to undo. I constantly told myself that I wasn't good enough, that I was going to hell, and I focused on past mistakes that I made. I spent so much time looking for bad in other people, I was naturally conditioned to look for the negative in myself, too. I wanted to understand who I was, and wrongly thought that picking myself apart would make me a better person. It doesn't.

Talking positively to yourself is one of the easiest and most natural ways to affect change in your life. The way we talk to ourselves doesn't just impact our relationships with ourselves, it also changes how we talk to other people. Would you ever let anyone talk negatively or use deeply hurtful language when speaking to you the way you talk to yourself? No, of course you wouldn't. You'd probably call it abuse, which is true.

By the time I was suicidal I had talked down to myself for decades and the self-abuse had gotten worse and worse, spiraling down until my mind was in a very dark place. That's how powerful what you say to yourself is. How can you ever get better if you're always countering the good things in your life with all of this negativity? I'm not saying it's easy to recode these habits, but it is very possible with small, consistent changes. You start by making a choice to stop talking down to yourself. Then every time you catch yourself saying something negative internally you pause and delete the negative thought from your mind, replacing it with a positive message to yourself. It won't happen all at once, but your thoughts will start to trend up instead of down, as the positive new coding becomes your preferred way of communicating with yourself.

The tone of how you talk to yourself is a major part of your self-review process. It's also one of the layers that's the hardest to peel away. It's impossible to be honest with yourself about you if you're drowning in negative self-reflection and can't see yourself objectively. Honesty isn't synonymous with harshness; you're more likely to experience a negative outcome if you're overly critical with yourself. You need to have a grounded, real understanding of where you actually are, not overly negative or positive, to see yourself accurately. Being self-critical won't make you a better person, it'll just drag you down. Truth in your life comes from balance.

Negative self-talk has a way of spreading to affect all areas of your life. Changing how you talk to yourself is a great way to change your code. Self-talk creates feedback loops, and those either amplify the good things or the bad things in your life. You can use this to your advantage to fix things that you're struggling with. Here's how to recode your life with reflective, positive self-talk. First identify a problem you know you have. Be reflective enough to identify just one area where you are using negative self-talk and turn it around. It might be your appearance, your job, your relationship, etc. Instead of beating yourself up over and over again, what if you use positive self-talk to change the messages you are sending yourself. Instead of cursing yourself for what's wrong in your life, give yourself constructive ways to make the change you want to see. Instead of beating yourself up, switch your focus to what you need to do to change the problem you've identified. You have to be proactive about it, building yourself up intentionally and reinforcing the positive self-talk until you believe it. Change is a whole lot easier when someone's building you up, not tearing you down, so be that person in your own life.

SHAPE YOUR THINKING

Self-review goes beyond how you think about yourself to understanding how your thinking affects your experience. The next challenge to master is controlling where you direct your thoughts. This is important for focus, so you can enlist your mind in specific tasks to create the life that you want. Directing your thoughts in ways that build you up every day help you to first envision and then take the actual steps necessary to create your desired life.

I have worked very hard to learn to control what I think. It doesn't come easily, it's a skill that takes time to master, but it's one that you don't lose once you have it. There is a freedom in realizing how much influence you can have in creating the life that you live and understanding how to limit the control others have over your life.

A great example of controlling your thoughts will help you maintain a trusting relationship and avoid the temptation to cheat. There's always going to be a beautiful woman or a handsome guy that's interested in you, even if you're in a relationship, almost everyone has dealt with this dilemma. It sometimes feels like you're more of a magnet when you're already attached. Pop culture makes it seem like infidelity in relationships is everywhere. I've experienced both sides of this problem. It's not something that I'm proud of, but it's something that I've learned to combat. Before it's even a thought, attraction is a feeling. So as soon as it starts to swell, just a tiny bit, I shut it down. I don't even allow myself to entertain the thought. This self-control isn't coming from my partner forcing me to act in a certain way, it's coming internally from me because I made a decision to commit to this person and to not look elsewhere. That first inkling of thought you have about an old girlfriend or boyfriend or the moment you catch a good-looking coworker looking over at you, just kill the thought to cheat. Don't even allow yourself to think about the individual in a romantic way, don't imagine what could be, and don't go stalk them on social media. Will your thoughts to move on to an entirely different subject. Cut the cord of dead weight in your mind dragging you down. You're not limiting yourself by controlling it, you're actually freeing yourself from the weight of things that will detour you away from your goals.

This strategy works in all kinds of situations, not just relationships. If you're trying to cut out ice cream from your diet, you have to train yourself not to think about ice cream. If you're trying to work out every day, you have to shut down all thoughts about skipping the workout. If you're working to keep your house clean, you have to push down the thought of not making your bed today. It literally does not matter what it is you want to do, if your mental capacity is occupied thinking ideas that are the opposite of what you want to accomplish, you're more likely to end up doing what you spend your time thinking about.

Using words like "I should," "I can't," or "I need to" all limit who you can be. You're teaching yourself either to trust or not trust yourself. Every change you successfully make will increase your confidence in yourself and your ability to create your ideal life. It all begins with choice and intention.

CONNECTING WITH EMOTION

Employing these skills helped me to improve the way that I thought about myself and I found that I could connect with my emotions more easily. For years I'd buried my emotions because that's what my father and the church taught me to do at our monthly priesthood meetings. My mom lived according to her feelings and emotions, but I was taught that it was wrong to live that way. Men were supposed to be stoic and protective. There was this huge, heavy burden placed on us to be upstanding and reliable fathers and husbands. To some men in the secular world, the idea of having a bunch of wives sounds great. The reality for men in the FLDS Church was that being responsible for several wives and dozens of children was a burden of responsibility. If you were following the church's commandments, sex wasn't to be used for pleasure, just for procreation, so polygamy wasn't the fun outsiders imagined it to be. Anyone who's been a husband or father realizes it's a massive amount of pressure to be the perfect protector and supporter to just one woman and child.

For me, learning how to connect with my emotional nature was tough. I spent a great deal of my twenties going from relationship to relationship because I was so emotionally disconnected. It wasn't just relationships with women, it was my relationship with myself, too. I wasn't able to have true self-reflection because I couldn't access my true emotional nature.

Some people, often men, are afraid of their emotions. It's no small thing to face who you are and potentially find things that you have repressed. After all, there are good reasons you've been ignoring these parts of yourself. Finding the path to emotional understanding and self-awareness can turn you into a better leader in your life, both personally and professionally. You make better decisions, you're more creative, and it's easier to collaborate with other people when you understand your emotional nature. It will also help you to become a better parent and partner. Whatever it is that's holding you back, it's not nearly as bad to face it as it is to live with it and let it take control of your destiny.

Identify three areas where you're planting weeds in your own garden.

What is one part of your life where you could do better with more positive self-talk?

Name one aspect of your emotional nature that you've identified in yourself.

What are areas of your life that you feel you can grow during the next year?

CHAPTER 11
ROUTINE

It's not what we do once in a while that shapes our lives,
it's what we do consistently.
- Tony Robbins

What you do every day determines who you are. It's the repeated things that happen again and again, not the big sweeping gestures, that matter the most. You can't move forward in your life if you haven't created a positive routine. The things that have been around the longest in this world are the ones that took the longest to make, that were worked on day after day after day. The Grand Canyon was cut by water that flowed across rocks for thousands of years every day slowly wearing the hard rocks away. Steady, repeated actions are what make your life what it is.

YOU ALREADY HAVE ROUTINES

Even if you didn't intentionally create a routine for yourself, you have habits that you engage in repeatedly. For instance, at the lowest point of my time drinking and partying I had established self-destructive routines that revolved around hanging out in bars or clubs. I fooled myself into thinking that I was living it up, wild and free spirited. The truth is that I was just repeating the same destructive behaviors over and over again. Go out, get wasted, come home, sleep, get up feeling hungover and trudge through work so I could go out and do it all over again. Where I partied or who I partied with and the specific things I did when I was partying might change, but it was still a routine. There was nothing exciting about it when you get down to it, it was just a big circular existence trying to escaping who I was inside my own head. It's easy to unconsciously get stuck on autopilot in routines that aren't working.

When you're a child, your parents determine your first routines. Parents work hard to establish these routines for kids to create stability. They include putting them to bed on time, giving them a feeding schedule, teaching them to brush their teeth every morning and night, etc. As kids grow up and become adults some reject sticking to a schedule, thinking they don't need structure anymore. That's crap, adults absolutely need the structure of a routine to be successful.

A lot of the routines from your childhood stay with you as an adult, stuck in your subconscious. When you think about your daily life, you'll probably find that there are a lot of habits you brought with you from your parents, whether you meant to or not. Perhaps you indulge in a routine of eating out, or clean your house in a certain way, or floss twice a day, you can likely trace those habits back to your childhood. Thought processes are routines too and also come from our upbringing. Sometimes you'll choose to keep those inherited routines in your adult life and in other cases you'll abandon them. That circles back around to self-evaluation, because you can only change your habits if you recognize what they are. Self-awareness is the key.

BROAD ROUTINES

People tend to think of routines as habits like making your bed every morning or waking up at a certain time. Yes, those are definitely routines, but they're the little version of routines. There are bigger, broader routines too. These are the things that arc through your life, repeated patterns that cause you to come back to the same problems over and over again.

Life is full of unexpected storms. Throughout my twenties, I had what seemed to me like storm after storm of the most stressful, life-changing events that can happen to a person. I left the FLDS Church. I married and divorced three times. My father died. I was hospitalized for a traumatic brain injury and long recovery. I jumped from job-to-job, changing careers completely at one point. I filed for bankruptcy. My son was born. Some of the things that I experienced were outside of my control, some were within my control and resulted from making the right decision, but most happened because I made outright stupid decisions guided by incorrect principles. I spent twelve years slowly declining, a downward spiral that I didn't fully realize was happening until it was out of control. All of these events led me to the suicide attempt that would finally wake me up.

Everyone goes through hurricanes in life that knock us down. Although I am now more self-aware, it's impossible to completely insulate yourself from tragedy. There are people I love that I will likely outlive, financial burdens will come, relationships will fall apart, and natural disasters will occur that turn my world upside down. Everyone knows people that seem to be incredibly resilient. They have problems in their life but they always seem to bounce back quickly and stronger than before. Their secret is they have learned to control their thinking. Not just their daily routines, but also their broader and larger habits.

In my twenties I had a consistent pattern of changing careers, religions, and relationships, desperately trying to find acceptance. After I left the FLDS Church, I got married, joined the Church of Jesus Christ of Latter-day Saints, and started a new job. I didn't stick with any of those things for very long because I was trapped in a routine of quitting when the people and things in my life no longer filled the void inside of me. I routinely looked outside of myself to try and find ways to feel whole.

My first marriage was to a woman that I met not long after leaving the FLDS Church. She was the first girl that I had ever really dated. Remember that I'd been coded in my childhood that it was normal not to know someone well before getting married. She and I dated for a year, broke up, got back together, and then married about the time my dad died. Losing him affected me in ways that I didn't anticipate. I felt out of control, like I'd lost my anchor, even though I was a grown man living on my own. Now that I am older and have perspective, I can see that my first marriage was an attempt to fill the hole caused by the loss of my father. I tried to drown my sorrows in alcohol and partying, and that's not a good recipe for a happy marriage.

My second marriage was to a woman who came from a close-knit family actively involved in the LDS Church. That's one of the things that drew me to her because I missed that close sense of family I had grown up with in the FLDS Church. The feelings of community and acceptance in that relationship were very important to me. I wanted to impress her family and convince them that I was the good man that I envisioned myself to be, so I joined her faith and she and I were married in the temple. This is a big deal in the LDS community because it bonds you not just for this life, but in the world beyond too. I wanted to be a part of something bigger than I was. For a while I thought I could really make this second marriage work, but I hadn't addressed my underlying problems or broken out of my routine of doing things just to be accepted. Ultimately, I couldn't be in a healthy relationship with my spouse or be solid in my faith, because I was looking, once again, for approval outside of myself. That's why that marriage fell apart, because I wasn't in it myself. I wasn't in it for myself. Of course I'm not going to get anything out of it.

After that marriage, I fell right back into my old daily routines again drinking heavily and becoming increasingly self-destructive. The same pattern was repeating itself and I was foolishly looking for a new woman to fix me. I mistakenly thought that if I just had the right woman by my side, she could solve all my problems.

Marriage was a major deal to me, because I had been coded from my childhood that it was the highest accomplishment to work for in life and the ultimate fulfillment for a man. I never wanted to be a polygamist, but I did believe in the FLDS Church's teaching that it was my job, as a man, to provide for and care for a wife and children. I held on to the belief that a family of my own would satisfy my need for unconditional love and acceptance. I'd been taught from my youth that the people you surround yourself with push you towards righteousness. After I left the FLDS Church, I wasn't as worried about being righteousness as I was about being happy and living a full life. Unfortunately, I didn't have any idea how to do that in a secular way and I made a lot of mistakes figuring it out. Some of the toughest times in our lives are self-made.

At this time in my life I thought that the secret to becoming the man I wanted to be was to put the right people in my path, so I married again. I met my third wife shortly after being injured in an assault. I was in a dark, turbulent place but we decided to have a child anyway; like a lot of relationships I thought having a kid would fix things. It never does. Having a child made things more stressful in an already stormy relationship. Children are wonderful and I wouldn't trade my son for anything, but having him didn't save our tumultuous relationship.

The upheaval of a third failed marriage and all of the other massive life changes in my twenties made me feel like I didn't have anything concrete to hold on to. The only pattern in my life was instability and there was a weird kind of comfort in that chaos because it had become familiar. Disordered and destructive, but predictable.

Routines give you a firm foundation so you can move forward in all areas of your life. You can respond to problems outside of your control a lot better if you have already mastered control of yourself by establishing healthy daily routines. This principle is even more effective if you're aware of your broader habits and have addressed and learned to break the cycle of repeating negative patterns in your life.

BITING OFF MORE THAN YOU CAN CHEW

When you get a handle on your daily patterns, you are empowered to take control of the larger routines in your life. One thing I learned during my time in the FLDS Church and escaping from its ideological hold on my life, is that positive habits are a big part of moving forward. I've learned for myself that if you have a goal to attain something you must make daily, small and important changes to accomplish that goal. Many people have the misconception that once they've decided to make a change, it will just miraculously happen. As if a fairy godmother will suddenly appear to fix all their problems with a wave of her magic wand. They want a get rich quick scheme or a crash diet because they like the idea of a fast fix and immediate results without doing the tough day-to-day work true change requires. The daily grind isn't glamorous, and it's not easy, but it's the key to permanently changing your code. The secret is recoding gets easier every day that you persist with your new routines. It takes longer, but when you have healthy routines in place making changes in your life aren't as difficult to implement.

You'll find that when you make small, daily changes to your habits, you're also reprograming your code in surprisingly powerful ways. Having solid routines reduces the need to plan, making life more efficient and freeing up more time in your life. Time is your most valuable resource. For example, years ago I felt like my energy was fluctuating throughout the day and I didn't have the focus I needed. When I realized my sleep schedule was the problem, I made the decision to wake up every single day at six in the morning. The body needs a set schedule, it's essential to being healthy and happy. Going to bed and getting up at the same time was a really simple change to make, but it's had a massive effect improving my productivity and feelings of well-being throughout my whole day and my whole life. It doesn't matter if I don't have to be at work until noon, it's a Sunday, or I'm on vacation, every single day I'm up at the same time. This routine gives me time to meditate, to exercise, and to eat a good breakfast with my son and spend time with him on the days that he's with me. I never miss my work out because I've made the time each morning for exercise because it's an identified priority for me. I'm not stressed because I'm never rushed. Each day starts out with the kind of peaceful reflection that I need to meet the challenges ahead and to make progress toward my goals. I don't stay out late partying anymore because I choose not to, my body is programmed to get up at six, so I don't want to stay up late.

This is one habit that I highly encourage everyone to adopt. Many hugely successes people like Steve Jobs advocate going to bed early and getting up early. It's not the time of day that makes the difference, it's the routine. If your job and lifestyle allow you to wake up at eight or nine every day just be consistent. Successful routines start by establishing habits for yourself that move you towards your goals.

You got where you are through habits and you'll get where you want to go by changing those habits, but it will take time. You won't make huge changes in one moment, so be patient with yourself when you are breaking out of old habits and creating new routines. People often set goals like "I'm going to lose forty pounds" and make ten changes all at once to accomplish that goal. They'll add a totally new diet, cut their calories down, and sign up for five spin classes a week. I've done this, we all have, and it's just not sustainable. After a week or two of exhaustion and starvation many fall right back into the old habits that caused them to put on the extra pounds to begin with.

Growing up I was a bean pole. By the time I was eighteen, I was six foot two and a hundred and fifty pounds. If I turned sideways, you couldn't see me. I wanted to bulk up so I ate everything I could get my hands on. That worked for a while because I was physically active, but over time my age caught up with me and my metabolism slowed. Suddenly I was in my thirties and weighed two hundred and forty pounds, overweight and miserable in my body. I wanted to change my body, so I started with just one change. I began consistently going to the gym five days a week. The specific exercises I did weren't important, I had developed a habit of going to the gym and that was the most important hurdle I recoded.

Once I had a habit of going to the gym, I made another small change adding a workout to my routine. It was easy, because I was already going to the gym five times a week. I started with a twelve week exercise program. I wasn't perfect at first, I'd miss a day and then get myself back on track. After a few weeks I started seeing some results and became more comfortable in my new habit, so at that point I was ready to make another small change and I began tackling my diet. Slowly at first, not all at once, I changed one meal a day. By being persistent and making small incremental changes, I experienced the results I desired and created lasting routines. After a year, my body and mind were in a totally different place. Not because of a crash diet or extreme exercise regime that weren't sustainable. Through small, consistent changes I made on my timeline, adding one new thing when I felt ready, I had recoded myself.

There will always be things that you can't change in your life, storms that pass over all of us like a parent dying, or a car accident. If you've got a strong routine established, healthy habits can support and help you to get through tough times. Learning to apply these principles to change seemingly insignificant routines will help you to change the bigger patterns in your life that you want to recode. You will learn that if you can change small things, you will be empowered to change big things in your life. I believe that's what we're all here to do.

Think about an instance where you bit off more than you could chew and it didn't work out well. How could you have made small changes so that things turned out differently?

Identify the broad routines in your life. What big themes do you see repeating?

What are some of the daily routines that you already have?

CHAPTER 12
GOALS AND GOAL SETTING

With self-discipline, all things are possible.
Without it, even the simplest goal can seem like an impossible dream.
- Theodore Roosevelt

At a certain point, I realized that I needed to be more deliberate in how I thought about my life. I needed to be specific, if I wanted to make a change. That's where goal setting came in.

It's a cliché to sit down with a goal book and create a vision for your life. There are a thousand self-help books out there that focus on setting goals and so many motivational speakers sharing their philosophies on goal setting that it can feel overdone. But there's a reason the self-help industry is a billion dollar business, people want to change and change is possible; goal setting works.

GARBAGE IN, GARBAGE OUT

Having vague goals is something we all do. We have an idea of what we want and then we start to go after it, but not always in a constructive way. People who want to go back to school start looking for the right program to apply for or school to attend. People who want to buy a car or a house start saving up by putting money in the bank.

People who want to find a spouse go out to a bar or download a dating app. We do small things without a clear view of what we want to accomplish. In my experience, without a detailed, specific vision, you are going to end up with whatever the universe throws in your direction. You can't put something vague out there and expect to get something specific back.

Let's say you want a really great meal, you want to taste the best steak of your life. Perhaps you had a great steak once before when you were on vacation and you know the specific flavor that you're craving. Now you want to be able to make it at home so it tastes just like it did at the fancy restaurant. If you buy a cheap cut of meat and throw it on the grill it won't taste like filet mignon. Even if you season it perfectly and cook it just right, it's still going to taste like a cheap piece of chuck.

Whatever you put into your life, is what you'll get out of it. You must identify specific goals to get what you really want in life.

GOALS ARE A WAY OUT

After my attempted suicide I realized that no one was going to save me; I needed to fix myself and create the life I truly desired. I was getting the same crap out of my life that I was putting into it. Not in terms of how hard I was working or how often I was trying, but all my efforts were focused in the wrong directions. My broad thoughts and vague ideas of what I wanted weren't the answer. Creating specific goals allowed me to wrestle control of my own life.

. I spent more than a decade of my adult life thinking that all of my problems were caused by other people. Change only happened after I realized that I needed to stop blaming others for everything that was wrong in my life, because it was never anyone's fault but my own. I knew that the problems were mine because even though people came into and out of my life, I consistently had the same issues. The common denominator was me. When I first realized that, it was incredibly scary and I wanted to run away from the realization. That's part of what drove me into such a deep depression, because I knew that I was my problem. I was torturing myself on a daily basis and I was the only one who could stop the self-destructive thoughts and behaviors. The crazy thing is this same realization is what pulled me out of the darkness. I understood that I had this huge amount of power to change my life for the better. My darkest point of despair became the brightest point of hope for me.

The simple act of writing down your vision for your life can be revolutionary. It changes you because it changes how you view the world. For me, my goals became the ladder I used to climb out of the pit of alcoholism and depression that I had felt trapped in for so many years. Even if you've tried to change your life before and failed, it doesn't matter. The difference is this time you have specific, clear goals that will help you to get back up when you start to fall back down into the pit you have dug through years of bad routines. You are going to fail. You are going to fall off the wagon. Nothing is instantaneous, not even with great goals and good intentions. That does not mean that your goals are meaningless or you aren't making progress towards them. Remember you're closer to where you want to be than you were when you started.

VISIONING

What is it that you want out of life? Not on a general level, because of course we all want happiness, money, love, those kinds of things.

What is it that you really want and does this look like in your life?

This starts from the top down with a vision, where your routines are meeting that vision from the bottom up. They come together in the middle to give you a purpose and a direction for your life that makes it all happen.

Visioning is big, broad strokes on the canvas of your life. You need a destination for yourself so that when you look back at the end of it you can see where you started in relation to where you want to be. Don't get too caught up in a fantasy vision for your life, but at the same time don't sell yourself short. Remember visions change. Your aspirations for your life today will not look the same in five years. You want it to change because you are always progressing and your life needs to grow with you. There is no such thing as "getting there", "finishing" or "the perfect life". When you embrace the changing nature of your life and understand how you grow personally, that's when you're going to find the true happiness you've been searching for.

Perhaps you've created vision statements in the past, but didn't find the exercise useful and are hesitant to try it again. That's a legitimate and understandable concern. This time will be different because you are using the principles of the Chi Code and will have the tools to realize your vision statement and create a different outcome.

A vision statement is written in first person and isn't long, it's just a paragraph. It sets out what you want your life to look like and should touch on all of the major aspects of who you are. Important parts of a vision statement include:

- Work/Finances
- Health/Physical
- Relationships

- Family

- Spirituality / Emotional Health

- Environment

- Learning / Mental Improvement

- Charity / Activism

- Fun / Entertainment

Here's an example of an early vision statement that I came up with for myself. Notice how it touches on these major points and puts intention behind them without getting overly specific. Later on you'll add specified goals that will move you forward and help you realize your vision.

"I am a successful speaker / coach and a published author. I have a perfect balance of work and personal life. I have an abundance of money which provides time, energy, and freedom. I am happily married to a beautiful woman who is the love of my life. We have a passionate relationship. We value each other's opinions and take great care in continuing to foster and grow our love for one another's happiness. We have children, and we keep them our main priority, encouraging them to find out who they are and to follow their dreams. We are a spiritual family that trusts in a power much greater than ourselves. We are always grateful for what we are given and put a great focus on giving back to those around us and those who come into our lives. We have fulfilling experiences as a family and as a couple. We are well-traveled and always seek to broaden our horizons. We are living our dreams."

Once you've created a vision statement of you own, the next step is to put it into practice. Every morning before you get going with your day and every night when you come home before bed, you should read you vision statement. This realigns your mind and brings into focus where you should be putting your attention and effort. More than the defined, small goals you set for yourself, your vision is the thing that will keep you going and on track to accomplish your goals. When you feel like you've realized most or all of your vision, or your ideas about what you want in life changes, you'll know it's time to create a new vision statement.

Every aspect of your life should be growing. Your vision statement gives it a direction to grow in.

BREAK DOWN YOUR GOALS

I have a very detailed habit of daily reviewing my vision statement. My goals change constantly, because there are always new things that I want in my life and new ways that I envision attaining my objectives. All new goals align with the vision that I've created for myself.

If your life is a car ride and you get in but you don't know where you want to go, then you will never reach your destination. Your vision will give you a destination, but your goals are the roadmap that will get you there. Most people don't even have a destination for their lives, so just knowing where you want to go, will put you ahead of the rest of the pack.

I create specific goals for what I want to do with my life. I break each goal down, from far out milestones a month or six months away, to the weekly and daily things that I need to accomplish to get there. I record myself talking about my goals, save the audio file on my phone, and then play it back to myself every day. Find out what works for you, whether it's posting them on your fridge or listening to your goals in the car. Doing this is going to keep you on track because you don't have time to do things that aren't aligned with your vision of your life.

For instance, after my third marriage ended I decided that I did not want to repeat my same mistakes, by meeting a woman and just falling into a relationship because it felt right in that moment. It took me being married to three women (not at the same time!) to realize that my actions were not aligned with my vision. Instead of just putting myself out there to find someone, I created a detailed list of what I wanted and didn't want in a partner. That probably doesn't sound very romantic, but it turned out to be the right way for me to meet the woman of my dreams. It forced me to not settle for someone who didn't fit into my life's vision, no matter how tempted I might be in the moment.

I look back to the period of my life when I was a young adult and had just walked away from the FLDS Church. I had no idea what I was doing, no goals, and no clue what I wanted out of life. All I knew, was that I didn't want to be under the thumb of Warren Jeffs. That's something, and it's not a bad something. Knowing what you don't want is important in helping you figure out what will bring you happiness. You have to know where you want to go to get there, and goal setting and visioning are the keys to recoding your life.

CHANGING YOUR CODE CHAPTER 12

What are some negative goals that you've moved towards through your habits in the last year? Even if you never wrote them down or intentionally created them.

What are some positive goals that you've moved towards in the last year? Even if you never wrote them down or intentionally created them.

Based on the information in this chapter, create a basic vision statement for yourself.

CHAPTER 13
UNLOCK THE SELF

*Things don't go wrong and break your heart so you can
become bitter and give up. They happen to break you
down and build you up so that you can be all that
you were intended to be.*

- Charlie Jones

Standing on my lawn in the middle of the night with a gun in my mouth, I felt there was no solution for the problems in my life, except to end it. This was rock bottom for me; below rock bottom, if there is such a thing.

I don't believe everyone has to get that low to start digging out, but every one of us must come to a tipping point where we are pushed to finally change our lives. The change doesn't happen all at once, but almost everyone has a turning point that changes the way they think about themselves. It's different for all of us. I've known drug addicts who didn't get there until they were sent to prison, and I've known parents who've had the realization the day their first child was born. It's a deeply personal part of everyone's journey.

There's a moment when you realize that you have to take control of your life, or there will be no going back. The hardest thing for me was that my life was a mixed bag, it wasn't all bad and so I didn't realize

I needed a complete change until it was almost too late. Yes, I was an alcoholic and deeply depressed, but I also had good things in my life like money in the bank and a son I love with all my heart, who kept me working to be a better father. It took me so long to get to that final, dark place, because the darkness creeps in gradually. Up until the point I attempted suicide, I'd had little revelations along the way, but nothing like what changed for me on that night. I finally realized that what I was doing, or trying to do, to be happy wasn't working, it was killing me. I had to let go of the ego that was holding me back and start from zero to begin my life over and create the vision I wanted for myself.

COVERING THE PAIN

Anything that's bad for you can turn into an addiction, whether it's drugs or television. It's important to realize that bad coping doesn't just manifest as alcoholism or gambling, it can be overeating, buying things you don't need. There are a million ways people try to escape from painful or unresolved feelings in their lives. When I started therapy after my suicide attempt, I began to realize everything destructive in my life was a way for me to avoid confronting some unresolved issues from my childhood. I didn't understand what I was avoiding at the time, I just knew that I was in pain and I needed a distraction from it. For me, distractions came in the form of alcohol, unhealthy relationships, and working all the time. My number one problem was that I was looking for external validation. I didn't realize that it should be internal.

There were times in my life I'd tried to make changes, but I wasn't fully committed to a vision for my life, and so I always fell back into my old self-destructive habits. At times we are compelled to make changes, but when the compulsion is removed, and we haven't died, we often revert back to the behaviors that contributed to our underlying issues. When an overweight person has a heart attack they are often motivated by fear to eat healthy, get on the treadmill every day, and abstain from alcohol. Six months later their doctors may be disappointed to learn they are scarfing down cheeseburgers, drinking beer, and skipping workouts. A personal vision can give you a reason to keep going as you daily do the hard work that true, lasting change requires.

The summer of my suicide attempt I was on a rollercoaster with alcohol. I'd binge drink then swear off alcohol completely. One afternoon I started having severe chest pain; it felt like someone had stuck a knife in my heart and was scraping it back and forth across my chest bone. The pain was so severe that I went to the hospital, convinced I was having a heart attack in my mid-thirties. The doctor diagnosed me with severe alcohol withdrawal instead. I'd been drinking so heavily that when I scaled my drinking back or tried to stop, it gave me the shakes and I became violently ill. That day in the ER changed my view of alcohol and I realized that I had to stop drinking, I knew it was time for a change. The alcoholism I thought I hid so well was obvious, and this trip to the ER convinced me, that I was dangerously close to doing irreparable damage to my body. For a young man, that's a scary prospect. I'd watched several of my brothers deal with addictions that threatened their lives. I wanted to be around to see my son grow up. Losing my dad in my early twenties brought havoc into my life and I didn't want that for my son. Laying in the hospital I realized if I didn't make some major changes, I was going to die prematurely. This experience was a wake-up call for me, I didn't have the willpower or skills to quit drinking immediately, but for the first time I was honest with myself in recognizing I had to make a change.

As long as you are alive, you have a chance to turn your life around.

There are no mistakes that you can't recover from. There's no point where you're a lost cause. When you fall off the wagon it feels like a defeat, but it's not. You're still further ahead than you were before you started.

I've learned to look at the whole arc of where I'm going. When I was drinking heavily I was heading in the wrong direction away from my desired final destination. Every time I tried to change, it was like turning and walking in the right direction. Even if it was just a few steps or only a short while before I got lost in a bottle again, I was still closer to the sober life I desired for myself than I was before I attempted sobriety. Remember, it's meaningful and important to go in the right direction for any amount of time. It's not the win, but it's a win.

YOU DON'T HAVE TO HIT ROCK BOTTOM

After I gained experience making and breaking routines, I realized I can recode myself in other areas of my life. Getting through tough times and confronting yourself and your deepest fears changes you. I believe people who have faced the worst in life come out stronger and fearless. That's true for me. I no longer feel controlled by anything outside of myself. I am in control of my life and my destiny. It's a freedom that I didn't think was possible when alcohol controlled me, but now I've found it, I can't imagine my life without it.

I don't believe that it's necessary to hit rock bottom to be able to transform your life. Those of us that struggle with some sort of addiction like drugs or alcohol might only wake up when we hit our heads on the rock at the bottom. Substances cloud judgement and distort reality. They turn off the fail safe switches that usually protect us from hurting ourselves. Substance abuse problems make you so numb that you may not be aware of how unhappy you are with your life.

Numbing doesn't just come through alcohol and drugs. People effectively numb themselves all the time through other vices that are equally addictive. Social media is addictive and food can be too. People become addicted to shopping or gambling, hobbies or cleaning their houses obsessively. Even working out and relationships can become numbing agents if someone is using them to ignore their responsibilities or run away from them. Responsibilities include taking care of yourself emotionally and physically. Any kind of behavior in your life that is numbing you is negative. If you have negative past experiences, you have to face them instead of running away from them. I ran away from hurtful experiences in my past numbing myself with alcohol, work and women.

Most people will struggle with their vices for a while, realize how unhappy they are making themselves, and choose to change. They turn their lives around on their own. The people who are in the middle are the hardest to reach; they haven't gotten to the point where they realize there's a problem yet. That's where I was throughout my twenties, living in a dangerous middle ground where things weren't bad enough for me to change my life. This middle ground robs you of the most important asset that you have in life: time. People spend years in limbo with their lives slipping away, and those are precious years you can't ever get back. They just hover experiencing moderate success, content to be mediocre. In these cases I'd say it's almost better to be reckless because that will precipitate you getting to a place that you must get out of quicker. A life without goals is a huge problem because there's nothing to guide you towards your vision for your life. When you're living without goals you'll do a lot more backsliding than you will when you set goals for yourself.

During my twenties I wouldn't take accountability for anything. When things went wrong in my life it was always someone else's fault. If I acted out or got upset, it was because my dad just died or my boss was being a jerk. If I got divorced it was because my spouse was too demanding or too passive. If I was struggling with my faith it was my new church's fault because it was too similar to the FLDS Church of my childhood that I had escaped. I didn't want to deal with the underlying issues so it seemed easier to push the responsibility off my shoulders and onto whoever or whatever was most convenient at the time. There is always someone else to put the blame on.

There are people everywhere like me, take a moment to honestly reflect on whether or not you might be one of them. If you are, don't despair. I changed, and you can too. The key to real change lies in realizing that you have control over yourself. All of the control to change your life lies within you. You don't have to hit rock bottom to turn your life around, but you must start accepting responsibility for your own life. The good news is although it's tough to take responsibility for your mistakes, it feels great to take credit for your successes.

BUILDING SELF CONFIDENCE

Whatever you attach your self-esteem to will be a big driver in your future. When you attach your self-confidence to things that are outside of your control, you will no longer have any agency or control over how you view yourself. To build self-confidence, it's important to take other people out of the equation.

If someone has chosen to commit to me and spend their life with me, does that make me worth more? No, this is a dangerous mindset to get caught up in. If an attractive and successful person is associated with me, that may make me feel attractive and successful for a while, but. It's easy to become too attached to another person and lose sight of yourself. Then when the relationship either hits a bump in the road or completely falls apart, you're left without the ability to put yourself back together. You've lost sight of who you truly are when you aren't a whole person on your own. It's impossible to sustain "you" when you are always losing yourself in someone else. Most people attach themselves to their spouses. I was married three times in the years after I left the FLDS Church before I hit rock bottom and figured out how to change direction and get off the wrong path. All three of these relationships were about me looking for someone outside of myself to give me self-confidence. That's not fair to ask of anyone and I take responsibility for the failure of all three marriages.

I thought my first marriage would fix all the problems in my life. I was young and stupid, and she and I fit together well enough that I thought I could make it work. My upbringing in the FLDS Church had taught me that the number of wives you had was a symbol of your worth as a man. I didn't want to be a polygamist, but in this first marriage I did bring with me the idea that a woman would create meaning and purpose in my life. It wasn't a conscious thought, just an internal drive that I didn't understand or recognize where it was coming from at the time. This first marriage inevitably failed and I started picking it apart to understand why we hadn't been able to make it work. I used every little thing as an excuse. My dad was dying at the same time the marriage was falling apart, and I didn't know how to deal with any of it. So I blamed my wife and dad and went to the bar. I told myself my wife was the wrong person for me and I shouldn't stay with her because being with the wrong person made me feel miserable. Everything and everyone was an excuse to go out drinking. I didn't have the self-awareness to grieve for my dad, face my failings as a husband, or admit that I was an alcoholic.

The second time around, I went looking for self-confidence in a beautiful woman whose family were devout members of the LDS Church.

Her parents were very involved in their faith, and she was a wonderful woman. I loved her, so I joined her church, we got married in the temple and I threw myself into trying to be a good LDS husband. We attended church events, went to Sunday services, and spent a lot of time with her family. I was sober for a time, because drinking is against the church rules and I really wanted to be a good husband to her and to build a life together. Her parents were strict, sometimes even harsh, but that was familiar to me from my upbringing. At first I wanted validation from them. Looking back I think that's because I thought, unconsciously, that approval from them would compensate for the acceptance I desired so desperately and felt I didn't receive growing up in the FLDS Church. I learned the hard way, at the expense of marriage number two, that it's impossible to find self-esteem outside of yourself.

I became what they call a "sober alcoholic" because I wasn't drinking, but I hadn't addressed or fixed the larger problems that had prompted me to drink in the first place. After I left the marriage, I also stopped going to church and I started drinking again. Eventually she and I reconciled and even lived together for a couple of years and almost got married again. But ultimately the relationship ended because I didn't have the tools to fix myself and my insecurities negatively affected how I treated her. This relationship is one that I look back on with a stab of deep regret because it was me alone that screwed it up. She was a good person, moral and trusting. I wanted to be with her because she embodied what I didn't have within myself. I started to notice a pattern, that I repeatedly tried to replace the people in my life, without fixing any of my underlying issues, so my problems kept coming back to haunt me.

The third time around I went in the total opposite direction of my first two marriages. I met a woman at work who was a partier. She let me indulge in things without making me feel guilty and I loved that freedom. Again, I was looking for validation outside of myself. She made me feel like all the drinking was ok, that I was ok even with all of my faults. I was at my most reckless when we were together.

One night my brother and I were at a bar drinking in Salt Lake City, just down the street from my house. He was talking to some girls, and I was drinking more than anyone ever should. Two guys who weren't with the girls but wanted to be got angry with us for talking to them. One of them head-butted me and a bouncer stepped in and broke up the fight, kicking the guys out. A few minutes later security at the bar also kicked my brother and I out of the bar too, and as we walked downtown towards my house, I saw the guys we'd had the altercation with and decided to confront them. I was off the rails drunk, wanted to blow off some steam, and was not thinking logically, I thought we'd just yell at each other but as we walked up, one guy said "you're gonna get your ass kicked," and I realized too late these guys were on a completely different level. I'd been in little scraps before, nothing major where anyone got hurt or the police were called. For all of my partying, I'd always been very careful never to cross certain lines. The next thing I knew, I was waking up in the hospital. Between walking up to confront the men on the street and the hospital I have no memory; there's nothing but darkness.

That night I didn't just get knocked out, my assailant stomped on my head after I was unconscious, over and over again. I suffered a Traumatic Brain Injury (TBI), and the doctors initially thought I'd have to learn to walk and talk again. I was lucky, I ended up only losing my sense of smell. It took me almost a year to recover from the assault, and I walked around in a fog, self-medicating with alcohol.

It was during this time that I became involved with the woman who would become my third wife. There's something to be said for someone who is there for you through a traumatic event, and she was. Just three months after I was attacked, she got pregnant and we had a child together. My son is the center of my universe. I found a lot of validation in that relationship, but it was all external. That's the problem. I still hadn't fixed myself, so I ended up going through the same cycle with her that I did every other time I got married. I wasn't happy because of things inside of me, I blamed my unhappiness on her, and there I was divorced for the third time before the age of 30.

My marriages all ended because they didn't solve my problems the way I envisioned they would. For the first dozen years after I left the FLDS Church, I had no self-confidence. It probably didn't look that way to people on the outside who saw me as a successful business-man. In many ways I had a better life than most of the people I knew who left the church, and I'm thankful for that. While I seemed to live a charmed life on the outside, inside I felt worthless because I inter-nalized everything people said about me. I hadn't learned yet that the only opinion that matters is what you say about yourself. You're the only person who's going to be with you from your first breath to your last. Not your parents, not your siblings, not your spouse, not your kids, just you. Learning to rely on yourself is where self-confi-dence comes from. It's a liberating feeling. If I had put a solid routine for myself into place, I would have been less affected by the people around me and ultimately more grounded as an adult.

FACING THE FEAR

Following my TBI, I lived with Post-Traumatic Stress Disorder (PTSD) for a couple of years. It's one of the life-changing experiences that taught me to face my fears, I learned changing the way I think had the power to change my entire world.

The first time I left the house after the attack, I was paranoid. I looked around every corner cautiously and jumped at every noise. You don't realize how much you take the sense of safety for granted that we have all become accustomed to, until it's gone. When I was attacked it shattered my confidence because I realized that I couldn't protect myself physically the way I always imagined I could. I was this big, tough guy, but I was also physically vulnerable. The TBI was a major contributing factor in my downward spiral. I didn't feel like myself for two years after the assault. I was shaken to my core and had to rebuild my self-image. At first I numbed myself with alcohol. There was physical pain to drown out, but also mental anguish. The men who beat me up were arrested and charged with assault. I spent over a year in and out of court, testifying against them. Anyone who has been through the judicial system knows it is brutal. You are forced to relive the trauma over and over in front of people who have no sympathy or don't believe you. It's emasculating for a man because you constantly question why you let this happen to you. If I hadn't been so drunk or hadn't pursued the men after we left the bar, perhaps I could have defended myself better or avoided the situation completely. I never imagined I'd be the victim of a crime, because I had this idealized vision of men as tough and able to take care of themselves. The man who stomped on my head so viciously was sentenced to prison for the attack, and years later I found his obituary, but knowing that he's dead doesn't change the imprint of that night on me. My fear didn't die with my assailant. I had to come to the realization that the only person with the power to change my fear, is me.

Having a child during this time did help to ground me. I had the same idea about children that I did about marriage that having a kid would be the solution to my problems, which wasn't fair to my son or myself. The added responsibility made my drinking worse, but it also forced me to focus on someone other than myself. I never partied or was reckless when he was in my care. It was one of the things I drew a hard line at and wouldn't cross, like cheating on a partner or breaking a law. After his mom and I split up, we shared custody so every other week I was with him, which required me to focus on someone else. Having my son pushed me to my absolute limits forcing me to face my fears. It also gave me the opportunity to relive some of my childhood through him without the influence of the FLDS Church. This was a time where my coding actually came in handy. My dad had always been extremely consistent with us and I emulated him in my parenting. I never missed a doctor or dentist appointment, a soccer game or a school function. The payoff in facing my problems to become a better father was big, and priceless: my little boy's smile.

Having a child isn't the solution to any problem, but for me, it helped to give my life a positive purpose. This only worked to help me turn my life around because I was also willing to do the internal work to face the demons that I feared from my past to create a better future for myself and my son.

What or who is your biggest motivation to make changes in your life?

What are the patterns in your relationships that have held you back in the past?

List the positive qualities that you bring to your life and relationships.

A WISE MAN ONCE SAID NOTHING.

CHAPTER 14
MEDITATION

We are shaped by our thoughts.
We become what we think.
When the mind is pure,
joy follows like a shadow that never leaves.
- Buddha

When we talk about the path forward, we first have to talk about the path that brought us to the present. Numbing yourself to escape from your feelings or pushing them down to a place inside yourself where you think they can't reach you is delaying the inevitable. They will eventually reach you. Meditation is a way to approach the feelings that you're avoiding and learn how to not be overwhelmed by them.

Meditation allowed me to stop dwelling on the past and gave me a place to start from in the present. As I continue to use it as a tool in my life, it lets me find a place of indifference for the things that I can't control. There is nothing in life worth having that you don't need to work for, and I've worked hard for the peace that meditation has brought to me. Changing your coding takes time and energy. There were moments of enlightenment that came along the way, but those were hard won battles, the culmination of my effort and life experience that went before them. Your past has to become integrated with your present when you make a conscious decision to change your coding to create the future you envision for yourself. It's tough, but it's definitely worth it. I never imagined that I could be who I am today, and it's meditation that got me here.

INTEGRATING THE PAST

The year prior to my suicide attempt I'd only drank alcohol three or four times, each over the course of a drinking bender that lasted a couple of days. I would consistently go three months and then have a two day relapse, then go back to total sobriety. I realized that I wasn't addressing the feelings that made me turn to alcohol and drink excessively each time I fell off the wagon. My life kept turning around in a devastating circle and I knew then that I had to fix the problem. I was in a downward spiral headed for rock bottom.

When I finally did stop drinking for good, after my suicide attempt, I started looking for ways to support my sobriety. I was determined not to fall into the same patterns that had trapped me before. The biggest change, the thing that actually turned my life around, was that for the first time I recognized that my problems were inside of me. Not only did I know that I was the problem, for the first time I believed I had the power to fix me.

Over the years I had gone through the motions of addressing my alcoholism and childhood issues. I'd seen six or seven therapists. I'd go to therapy for a while, talk about the immediate problems happening in my life like my current relationship, or the stress from work, or the traumatic brain injury. They all focused on the problems that I was facing in my life at the moment I was talking to them. No therapist ever discussed the issues from my past, not in any amount of detail. Our sessions only focused on the here and now, like my past didn't matter or contribute to my current problems.

I saw a neuropsychologist after my head injury. I was comfortable unloading about everything and so I did, and it seemed to help, at least for a little while. But eventually my problems would resurface and come crashing down on me again. I didn't understand why. Going to therapy was tough and I was doing the hard stuff that guys are supposed to be afraid of doing like talking about my feelings, so why wasn't it working? Next I read dozens of self-improvement books, met with the big names in the self-help industry, and took their seminars. I tried meditation a couple of times and tried to improve my spirituality by being active in my church, but nothing ever stuck. I ended up in the same situation again, causing my level of frustration to climb, and fueling my drinking. It's tough to stay positive when you think you are doing everything right, but your life continues to go wrong.

After my suicide attempt I felt I needed to find a new therapist. I looked for someone who would bring something different to the table, who could give me a different perspective on my issues. Albert Einstein is widely credited with saying, "The definition of insanity is doing the same thing over and over again, but expecting different results." Under this definition I had been insane my entire adult life. I was ready to break the cycle. I chose an older therapist who as near retirement and came highly recommended, I walked into his office and told him I didn't want to talk about my present issues, I wanted to confront my past. A short while into the session, he asked me if I'd ever tried hypnotherapy. I decided to give it a try. The beauty of this process was that I'd never talked to this man about my past before he put me under hypnosis. This made the whole experience and my resulting insights feel a lot more real to me.

In the session my therapist took me into a hypnotic state, where I walked towards a chalkboard and stood in front of it. He told me that the answers to his questions would appear on it. He asked me when it was that I felt abandoned as a child, because my drinking, partying, anger, and recklessness were all childish actions. On the chalkboard the number four appeared. Then he told me that we were going to go find my four-year-old self. I walked down a hall and eventually came to the door where I knew I would find myself. The door opened to the outside, and there before me was my childhood home. On the front porch was a little boy with blond hair and blue eyes, just as I had looked when I was that age. The child was quietly crying, his head buried in his hands. The therapist told me to pick up the child and tell him that I'd be his protector from now on. I took the little boy into a room inside, made him comfortable on the couch and sat next to him. I talked to him and comforted him. Then I gave him a phone and put a screen on the wall in front of him. I told him that he could see me on that screen any time he wanted to, and that he could call me on the phone if he ever needed me. The four-year-old me would let me know if I was acting out. The therapist then had me leave and come back to the real world.

It seems almost silly, but I felt a great wave of relief after that first session. Like I'd experienced a breakthrough. I didn't really believe that this brief episode would create a major shift in my life, but the next day while I was driving through rush hour traffic I was able to test it out. I felt the familiar swell of road rage towards the people driving like idiots and the emotion started to take me over, the way it always did, and then, just as suddenly as it started, it just stopped. I felt my four-year-old self pop up inside my head and immediately my childish anger just ebbed away. It was a confirmation that I didn't expect, and from that moment on I was better able to handle my wild emotions.

During the next session, the therapist took me into another hypnotic state. Like the time before, I ended up in front of a chalkboard waiting for the answer to his question "when did you feel the angriest in your life?" The number fourteen appeared on the chalkboard this time. I was fourteen when the FLDS School shut down and my parents sent me to work with the polygamist construction company. Again, the therapist directed me down a hallway to meet with my fourteen-year-old self. I found a young man who felt angry and abandoned, like his parents must not love him because they sent him away to work at such a vulnerable age. Again my therapist had me do the same thing, setting up a room for my younger self and telling the young man to call me if he ever needed me.

Those two events were formative experiences in my childhood. Moments that would shape the rest of my life and that I had never recognized or dealt with. Just because you don't deal with something, doesn't mean that it simply goes away over time. My therapist taught me how to go into the hypnotic state by myself, so that I could go and talk with these younger versions of me anytime. It proved to be very helpful to me in ways I couldn't have imagined and was another turning point in my life.

My therapist had been practicing for a long time and was retiring soon. In our final appointment, he took me under hypnosis again so that we could join all three ages together. During that hypnosis session we merged the four-year-old me, the fourteen-year-old me, and my present adult self. After that session, all of my animosity towards my parents from my childhood just disappeared. I didn't get the long-awaited apology from my mother or Warren Jeffs. I didn't talk to my dad one last time or hear some kind of explanation from Donna. I didn't need apologizes or explanations, I was at peace. Hypnotherapy might not work for everyone, but it worked for me. I finally understood my heartbroken four-year-old self was siloed off from the rest of me and would come out when I was afraid. My angry fourteen-year-old self was also separated and would emerge when someone upset me. . Recognizing what the true problem was helped me heal from my past and integrate the fearful and angry parts of me back into myself where I could better regulate them as an adult. Now that I was a whole person, I could live in the present no longer haunted by my past. My childhood coding wasn't something that I was afraid of anymore, by understanding how these experiences impacted me I now had the tools to recode my life and control my adult experiences.

Hypnotherapy helped me understanding that I needed to look inside myself to fix the problems in my life. I also found Jordan Peterson's Self Authoring Program very useful, which encourages you to break your life down into sections and write extensively about your most prominent memories. It was a lot of work to comb through my life, piece by piece, because there were so many things that happened to me. I invested a lot in myself so that I could make things right and find peace, for me, not for anyone else.

PEACE OF THE MIND

Once the breakthroughs with my past were addressed, I needed to incorporate the peace of mind I'd discovered into my everyday life. With hypnotherapy I'd cleared my garden of all its weeds, which was wonderful and amazing, but wouldn't last unless I kept pulling weeds. It's impossible to overemphasize the importance of routine in life; if you want to make a lasting change you must adopt a routine of daily mental weed pulling.

I'd heard about meditation for many years. After I stopped drinking the self-help books I was reading advocated "meditation, medita-tion, meditation." I didn't find any really good instructions in these books on how to meditate well. I tried guided meditations, but the twenty minute sessions felt like an eternity to me and I dreaded doing it and couldn't stick with it. From everything I read, that wasn't how it was supposed to feel and I couldn't figure out why it wasn't working for me.

For a long time, I'd listened to Howard Stern religiously. I found him to be insightful and funny, always pushing boundaries, but not the kind of guy I'd ever expect to get spiritual advice from. One day out of the blue on his radio program Stern started talking about Transcendental Meditation (TM). I remember thinking, this is not the type of guy who talks about this kind of thing. If I had heard Oprah talking about it, it probably would have gone in one ear and out the other for me, but hearing it come out of this lewd, crude, shock jock's mouth, caused me to take note and listen. Stern said TM was the key if you really want to be happier and in control of your thoughts. That was the first time I realized there are different kinds of meditation. So I set out determined to find a place to learn it.

TM is a non-profit organization with a methodology different from other meditation techniques. It's proprietary, so you won't read the secrets here, but it was life changing for me. I found a teacher in Salt Lake City and paid him a thousand bucks to learn TM for myself. What he taught was simple and easy, but in the first session I very clearly remember thinking "this is insane." I gave it a try despite my initial hesitation and I was so impressed with the clarity it brought that I've done twenty-minute TM sessions twice a day ever since.

Honestly, now it's second nature for me and I feel like I'm always kind of hovering around a meditative state. Occasionally things will still get under my skin and I'll get stuck in a situation that bothers me, but it never lasts for long. All the daily annoyances that used to bug me just don't matter anymore. I realize I create feelings of being upset in my own head and it's pointless. We've all seen movies about monks up on a high mountain who are enlightened. The hero climbs up seeking knowledge, but the monk's response is always the same, "The answer is whatever you think it is." They know that none of life's problems really matter, and you have the answers already. Before I learned meditation and the peace that comes with it, I would arrive home from work each evening completely stressed out by partner relationships, family relationships, bills, etc, stressors that we all deal with in our lives. I disagree with the prevailing misconception that it's impossible to rid yourself of stress, the best you can hope for is to manage it. It is possible, I've done it.

Once you realize this truth and believe it, it will help calm your mind. When stressful things come up ask yourself, "Does this really matter? Why am I doing this? Do I want to be a part of this and why?" Then you get the chance to make the determination for yourself, without the influence of anyone else. Your parents, your teachers, your boss, the truth is everyone is just as lost and scared as you are. Warren Jeffs and the leaders of the FLDS Church seemed like they had all the answers when I was a child but now I'm adult I can see they were even more lost than I was. People everywhere are just as insecure and out of control as you are, they are just better at faking self-confidence and certainty. There is no guru, no church leader, no romantic relationship or parental bond that can make the feelings of chaos inside of you go away. The only way to make it stop is to understand that whatever your stressor is, in the big picture it doesn't matter. When I started meditation, I began to understand how my worries were weighing me down and as I learned to release my stressors, I actually felt physically lighter.

The most important part of meditation is the habit of it. Once you learn the technique, you must have the discipline to sit down and do it for twenty minutes. No different from working out or writing a book, it's the routine that matters.

I tend to overthink a situation by mentally evaluating fifty different possibilities for how it could turn out. That was the biggest roadblock for me when I first tried meditation. I could not turn my thoughts off. That's why I drank, I was trying to shut my mind off with alcohol. Meditation taught me to shut my mind off in a healthy way. After you get the hang of it, you realize that nothing is worth getting stressed out over. Really, that's true of everything, none of it matters. People sometimes get confused when I phrase it that way, because it makes it sound like I don't think things are important. The point I'm trying to make is that we don't just go with the flow enough. You have to learn to take the good with the bad, the hard times with the good because worrying won't change the situation. We want to believe that we can control the way our lives go, but that's an illusion. We must interact with people every single day and we can't control what they do or how their decisions impact our lives. We can control our minds and what stressors we allow to impact our lives. Stress is such a waste of energy! Meditation helps you to get to a state of mind where you realize that all the stressors in your life really don't matter. Then you can stop worrying about things outside your control and refocus that energy into manifesting your positive vision for your life.

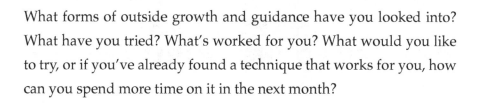

What forms of outside growth and guidance have you looked into? What have you tried? What's worked for you? What would you like to try, or if you've already found a technique that works for you, how can you spend more time on it in the next month?

Identify three things outside of your control that are current stressors. For each of the three things ask yourself, "Does this really matter? Why am I doing this? Do I want to be a part of this and why?"

What are three positive things you could focus time and energy on that will help you reach your vision for your life?

CHAPTER 15
CENTERED ON SPIRITUALITY

Persistence and endurance will make you omnipotent.

- Casey Neistat

Meditation helped me to realize that even after I left the religion that I was raised in, I could still have a relationship with God.

For so long, I'd thought that spirituality was a black and white, all-or-nothing choice. Either you were in the church and saved or out of it and damned. Through meditation, I realized that my connection to God was outside what any human could determine. God was beyond man's rules and judgements, limitless.

Religion and spirituality are not the same thing; God can be at the center of your life outside of a formalized system of faith and worship. Your relationship with Him is personal.

FIGHTING THE URGE FOR VALIDATION

We all have a need to be validated, it's a part of the human condition. As children we seek parental affirmation and rely on adults to tell us when we're doing the right thing and to reprimand us when we aren't. Children naturally want the approval of their parents and problems can arise when kids don't get the validation they desire and instead look for it in the wrong places. By the time you're an adult, you shouldn't need someone constantly telling you that you're ok. It's nice to receive affirmation from external sources from time to time, but it's essential to have internal self-esteem to carry you through your life.

I spent years of my adult life seeking the validation that I felt I missed out on as a child. Because of my religious upbringing, spirituality was a big part of that need for external validation for me. I looked for external sources, like a church, friends, family and relationships to save me. Years of running around, trying to please others so that they would validate me to try and make myself happy.

When I did finally break free of this fallacy, I could see the truth that had been there all along, that everything I wanted and needed could be found within myself. I was ignoring the one thing that I was in control of: me. Once I fixed myself, all of my other problems went away. Family, religion, career, money, they all fell into place when I made peace with myself. Once I focused on changing me and fought the urge to seek validation outside of myself every aspect of my life improved. You have ultimate control over yourself, and that gives you control over how your life goes. It's an illusion that someone else can fix aspects of your life you're dissatisfied with. No one can fix any of it but you.

This goes for spirituality too. No one can create a relationship with God for you. Not a preacher or a priest, not a shaman or a wise man. Yes, you can learn from people who have been down their own spiritual paths, but they cannot hand you a connection to the Divine. That's something that only you have control over. This was a major realization for me, because it was so ingrained in me growing up in the FLDS Church, that when prayed I wasn't entitled to personal revelation from God, that only came from the prophet. Religion was very public with mandatory acts of service, speaking in front of the congregation, following the religious laws in public by dressing a certain way and obligatory donations. I finally asked myself whether doing those things was to create a connection with God or to get external validation from the religious community around me. It's not an easy thing to figure out, because the motivations could be time and careful thought to understand the origins of my need for external validation. Recoding my need for validation from external to internal allowed me to develop a personal relationship with God and better understand how to effectively communicate with a higher power though meditation.

When Jesus instructed his follower to pray to God always, perhaps he was referring to meditation. I know when I began the regular practice of meditating, it gave me the confidence to understand that I didn't need outside validation and the answers to all of life's questions can be found inside of me. The clarity of meditation is a peace I carry inside of me all the time.

FALLING INTO THE TRAP

I believe the afterlife is a place where you're going to be your own judge. I don't think St Peter will be sitting at the pearly gates with a gavel, we are going to damn ourselves or redeem ourselves with the actions over the course of our lives.

Throughout my twenties, I damned myself. I made a lot of bad choices and hurt a lot of people because I was filled with self-hate and didn't know or like who I was. Now my life is different and I feel differently about myself. I've escaped the vicious cycle of self-loathing that pushed me into dark places and made me a slave to my addictions. I have a very different view now about what is important in life.

The universe, or God, or whatever it is that you want to call it, doesn't care about all of the materialistic and social pursuits in our lives. This is something I believe down to my core. We create all of this stress and drama, and in the eternal scheme of things none of it matters. The obligations and distractions that we pile on ourselves here don't even register with the beings that are beyond us. It's all an illusion that we create and propagate that's really just misdirection from the things that really matter like the knowledge we attain, the relationships we foster, and the legacy we leave for the next generation.

When people ask me what the secret to life is, I want to shout it out to them from the rooftops. It's a realization that I learned in meditative practice that transformed my relationship not only with myself, but also with the Divine. Don't lose yourself by letting people outside yourself define you. Learn and internalize the reality that life doesn't matter. There is no great secret to connection with God or to finding your life's purpose. It's so simple, you already know it. You've just fallen into the trap of thinking that you have to look outside of yourself to find it. You don't. Like the guru at the top of mountain says, "The answer is what you think it is."

INDESCRIBABLE PEACE

There is a peace that comes through self-reflection that's indescribable. I wish that I could share it with you right now, just put it into your heart through the pages of this book. That's not how it works though, which is probably for the best. The journey to get to a place of internal peace doesn't have shortcuts, you alone must do the work to find your chi. When I come out of meditation, or prayer if you want to call it that, I'm almost sad. It's definitely a bittersweet feeling. I have a peace in meditation, that doesn't persist outside of the session. During meditation you're beyond the harsh things and troubled times in your life. They cannot touch you because they are not real. They still aren't real when you come out of your meditative session, but they feel closer.

Life is not real when you meditate. What's real is the grounded and hard truth of that integrated experience. It's the only time when you are truly awake. The rest of our lives we are walking around and interacting, distracted by the things that aren't real and don't matter. In many ways, that makes life the real dream.

The real world is bustling with things all vying for your attention. These things distract from real existence, which happens when distractions fall away. People like Warren Jeffs create distractions, convincing people that obedience to commandments and edicts fosters spirituality. They don't. Distractions are the path away from peace. You'll never get to a place of fulfillment by following someone else's strict rules. I figured out that this indescribable peace was there waiting for me all along, locked within myself. Once you do find internal peace for yourself, it's not like anything you've ever felt before. The journey is miraculous, come find your chi.

MASTER OF THE SHIP

Spirituality is interconnected with routine. We are beings with souls, but the human bodies that we live in and the human brains that we have wired in our skulls demand consistency in order to attain freedom. Understanding routine helped me to overcome my alcohol addiction. Consistency made it possible for me to reshape my financial life. Habits allowed me to mold my body through diet and exercise. Consistent meditation opened up my emotional and spiritual life to a healthy and whole place.

It was a combination of consistency and a willingness to go deep into difficult things that I was afraid of that empowered me to make my life bright again after dark times.

Routine is going to give you the closest thing to control possible in life. It's easy to think that we control our circumstances, but we don't. We think that we are masters of our own ships, but that's a great illusion. All you have control over is how you handle each situation. Your reaction is what you need to learn to master.

Patience, with yourself, even more than with other people, will help you to become the real master of your life. It's a wonderful attribute, if you can acquire it. Things out of your control will happen every single day. We get upset over things we can't control like sitting in traffic. The reason that you're feeling mad is because you think that you should be able to go more quickly than you are. Once you realize that you have precisely zero control over things like traffic, that's the moment you become totally free. You cannot control how fast the cars are going, but you have absolute control over how you spend the time sitting in your car. Suddenly, your daily commute becomes an opportunity. You can listen to something motivational, or sit still and breathe deeply, you can call someone you've been meaning to talk to, the possibilities are endless.

Once you realize that the only ship you are the master of is your mind, it becomes easier to accept things for what they are. It's freedom, not unlike putting your life in the hands of God, only in this instance you get to participate through your autonomy by governing yourself. Personal autonomy is the capacity to decide for oneself and pursue a course of action in one's life. If that isn't the ultimate gift from God, I don't know what is.

What are the times in your life that you've felt most at peace? How did you get there?

What are the ways that you're the master of your own ship? List places that you feel in control and places that you feel out of control.

EVENTUALLY YOU'LL STOP CALLING THEM COINCIDENCES AND REALIZE HOW POWEFUL YOU ARE.

CHAPTER 16
THERE IS NO
MOUNTAIN TOP

*I am the wisest man alive, for I know one thing
and that is that I know nothing.*
- Socrates

For many years I thought that I knew the right way to live. Coming to the realization that I didn't know anything about what I wanted or who I was, changed me. Even when I recognized I was going down the wrong path, I always had a cockiness about me. I wanted everyone to think that I was in control. That phoniness was the worst thing for me because it delayed my personal awakening while I wasted years worrying about what others thought of me. When my alcoholism was at its worst, I would get sober for a couple of days and think that I was in control and didn't really have a substance abuse problem. I'd always relapse because I didn't do the work to get to the root of my drinking. This lack of self-awareness is dangerous, it almost killed me. The truth is no one who is growing is ever going to be comfortable.

You must get to the point where you realize that there is no end to your journey of self-discovery. There is no final destination you will arrive at, no summit to the mountain you are climbing. Instead, each new milestone offers a change in perspective, a different way to view the world and how you fit into it.

The journey is the goal, so live every day to its fullest. Living in fear of what may or may not happen when you die is no way to live. You deserve better than to constantly fear death and hell. No one deserves to live like that.

WHERE YOUR WORTH COMES FROM

Warren Jeffs measured his worth in wives. When his own weren't enough to satisfy his self-esteem, he took his deceased father's wives. That still didn't fill Jeff's self-worth void, so he married more women and then started taking younger wives until he was marrying twelve-year olds. Jeffs' relentless quest for self-fulfillment landed him alone, behind bars serving out a substantial prison sentence.

Everyone measures their worth in different ways, money, social status, level of education, earning potential, etc. I learned the hard way I was filling my void with mind-numbing alcohol and seeking self-worth in the wrong relationships. I experienced a breakthrough when I finally admitted to myself that I was measuring my worth in ways that weren't helping to make my life better or happier.

Today, being a good father to my son is a positive way that I find self-worth. It isn't just about having a kid I can show off. For me, the quality of parent I am to him gives me fulfillment and I take great pride in his progress and accomplishments, My self-esteem comes from being there for my son and knowing that I'm trying to be the father that he deserves. I had a great example in my dad who showed me that a man is always there for his children. In my tumultuous childhood, my father provided consistency and I've tried to continue this legacy for my son. Being a good father, one who's involved and present, is a priority in my life.

I also find self-worth in working hard. Working construction when I was fourteen was tough, but when I look back it definitely solidified my work ethic and taught me resilience and consistency. I believe this was why I was able to maintain and excel at jobs, even when I was an alcoholic. My work ethic is a major point of pride for me.

I don't cheat. Ever. My honesty and frankness are qualities that make me feel good about who I am. It's helped me to become a very successful salesman, because people know they can trust me and I won't lie to them. A large part of my self-esteem stems from my honest nature.

In order to grow, you must be more honest with yourself about what is good in you than what you need to fix. There needs to be balance. Part of my motivation to embrace spirituality was a need to seek out good things to help me recover from the bad experiences in my past. Too often people focus on what's wrong within themselves when they should be focusing that energy on developing what's right and good within them.

YOU'RE EITHER GREEN AND GROWING OR RIPE AND ROTTING

If you're not going in the right direction, then you're heading down the wrong path. There is no middle ground, no sitting on the fence, or straddling the line. In life, there's not really even rest stops; when you're sitting still, you're going backwards. Being complacent is dangerous, getting stuck in your comfort zone isn't a great place to be if your goal is progression. Individuals who push themselves consistently create better lives for themselves.

This is a skill you can teach yourself, here's how I did it. When I was twenty years old just a year or so after I left FLDS Church I bought a Tony Robbins Program. I knew that there was more to life out there for me and that the world was bigger than the small town where I grew up. I had lived in a world of secrets where things were done in the dark and no one ever explained their rationale for their actions. I was told what to do or not to do by religious leaders and instructed to never question their directives. The world opened up for me when I stepped out of the FLDS Church. I worked through self-help programs and read books constantly trying to figure out how to move forward with my life outside of the religious community. It wasn't until years later in hypnotherapy that I realized I had to look back and make peace with my past to move forward and live the future I envisioned for myself.

If I had a time machine I don't know that I would change any major event in my life. It's been a hard road, but I like where that road has led me and I like who I've become. I'm grateful to be where I am today. My own pain has formed me and I've become stronger, forged through the fires of my life. I'm not afraid to look at my life honestly and to take responsibility for the good and bad things growing in my garden. There was a long period of my life when I felt like a piece of fruit rotting and decaying on the ground, but now I feel like I'm back on the vine again. It's a good place to be. I am growing, not rotting.

There are cycles in everyone's lives. Ups and downs that challenge us and periods when you feel like you aren't growing anymore. If you have good people in your life they will try to help you, but ultimately you must help yourself. This book is designed to give you a starting place. It can show you the possibilities, but it cannot make you change your life. I've shared my story in the hope that you will be inspired by it and empowered to choose to make changes in your own life and recode your routines to live a centered chi life.

Living your personal vision for your life is hard, but it's real, it's possible and it's right here waiting for you. Make small, consistent changes to your routine every day, and you'll see rewarding benefits over time. It takes years for a tree to bear fruit. It's the same thing with people. If you tend your garden well and do the work to pull the weeds, your life will bear fruit too.

CHANGE YOUR CODE

My experience is probably totally different than yours. The thing that we share in common is that we are both coded with certain behaviors and life views. Even if you grew up in a more open environment than I did without the severe religious programming, rules and regulations that were normal for me, your coding is just as impactful on your life as mine was for me.

I look back over my life so far and I see a constant effort to make myself a better man. I failed often, at times I had poor judgement I can trace back to my childhood coding. I no longer blame my parents, the FLDS Church or even Warren Jeffs. Holding on to all the hurt and anger from my past isn't going to help me progress today. Whatever is holding you back from your past, recognize it and release it so it no longer has the power to affect your present in negative ways. It's never going to disappear from your memory, but by facing it and overcoming it through meditation, you can make past traumas work for you to help you understand your coding and recode your life for the better. I speak from experience. I've tried it both ways, letting my past rule over me in negative ways and letting go of my attachment to the past to embrace the present and create a new future. It's much better to let it go.

The people who stayed trapped in the FLDS Church, like my father and so many other family members and friends, they couldn't let go of the things that were hurting them. Spirituality is a beautiful thing, but when it's used as a weapon it becomes ugly. Many of the people I've lost to suicide or addiction were abused and destroyed through a twisting of pure religion into a tool of manipulation. My experience hasn't jaded me against all faiths, but it did help me realize that I have to break the cycle of abuse I grew up in. FLDS Church leaders took religion and used it to exercise power over good people and exploit their trust. They broke up good families and broke good people, but they didn't break me. Getting out from under my childhood coding is a mountain I'll climb for the rest of my life, but it's a journey I'm happy to be on.

Along the way, there were people that I had to leave behind. Negative people in your life have to be cut loose if they are holding you back. It's hard to tell family or friends that you can't have them around, but if they drag you back into old habits and routines you are trying to recode, you have to keep them a safe distance away where they can't negatively influence you. The journey is yours alone to walk; you don't owe it to anyone to stay in their lives if they threaten your climb up the mountain of self-discovery.

Everyone has to make their own way towards self-realization. If you're trapped in the cycle of where you started, unable to break out of your self-imposed cage, then your life will be limited. Take the good things that your family and your upbringing brought to you, and let the rest go. Having trauma in your past does not make you broken, incapable of happiness, or inherently worth less than anyone else. Through the painful work of self-reflection I learned that I could be strong, even in the hard times, you can do the same work and experience personal growth too. Don't expect it to happen overnight, remember there is no destination here, only forward motion. Start moving forward today.

You don't deserve to live a life that you didn't chose for yourself. You deserve to have the life that you want. It's up to you to break the code.

In Chapter 12 on visioning I shared an early personal vision statement I created for myself after I hit rock bottom and decided to change my life. It read, "I am a successful speaker/coach and a published author. I have a perfect balance of work and personal life. I have an abundance of money which provides time, energy, and freedom. I am happily married to a beautiful woman who is the love of my life. We have a passionate relationship. We value each other's opinions and take great care in continuing to foster and grow our love for one another's happiness. We have children, and we keep them our main priority, encouraging them to find out who they are and to follow their dreams. We are a spiritual family that trusts in a power much greater than ourselves. We are always grateful for what we are given and put a great focus on giving back to those around us and those who come into our lives. We have fulfilling experiences as a family and as a couple. We are well-traveled and always seek to broaden our horizons. We are living our dreams."

When I wrote down the life I wanted for myself my vision did not resemble my actual life in any respect. I was a thrice divorced, alcoholic, single dad working long hours as a salesman to support my drinking habit and son. At the time I had no public speaking experience and an ninth grade education, so the prospect of writing a book was daunting to me. I felt spiritually numb from the alcohol and the emotion baggage I had repressed from my strict religious upbringing in a cult. I didn't have the time, energy or money to put into service for the causes I believed in and I longed for fulfillment, peace and connection.

Despite all the seemingly insurmountable obstacles in my way, the one thing I did have going for me was a dream, a clear vision of what I wanted my life to be. That was the catalyst that helped me take the first step towards changing my life. Daily while I meditated, I focused on my vision for my life. My thoughts informed my actions and slowly, but steadily, the small, incremental changes in my habits created new, healthy routines. Each success empowered me to take the next step until what started out as a dream became my reality.

With the completion of this book, I will be a published author. As The Chi Code website gains popularity, so do my public speaking and coaching opportunities and I find incredible personal fulfillment sharing the principles that have changed my life as I travel and meet with people all over the world. My career has given me the financial security and freedom to give back to likeminded organizations and causes I believe in and bless the lives of others. I am grateful for a healthy body and clear mind, free from the influence of all addictive substances. For me, the fourth time was the charm. I am happily married to a beautiful, brilliant woman who is the love of my life. We enjoy a passionate relationship and as we both work to foster the other person's happiness, our love continues to deepen and grow. We talk to each other for hours and value each other's opinions, taking great care to support each other in our separate and shared goals. My wife is a wonderful influence in the life of my son and we are excited to grow our family with another child on the way. We agree our family will be our priority as we encourage our children to create and pursue their dreams, like their parents before them. Our family's foundation is our spiritual belief in a higher power and we seek truth to broaden our horizons. I can honestly say we are living our dreams.

My personal vision statement isn't complete with the realization of these goals. I am just getting started. I challenge you start with me, let's take the first step together.

CHANGING YOUR CODE CHAPTER 16

How do you measure your worth?

What can you change to help you get where you want to go in life?

What's your biggest takeaway from this book?

What's the next step that you're going to take to change your code now you've finished this book

EPILOGUE

The end is only a beginning in disguise.
Craig D. Lounsbrough

The end of this book isn't the end of your journey, or of mine.

What comes next is up to you, because you're the only one who can make a change in your life. My life continues to grow and change, in good ways and in challenging ways. I'm excited to see what's ahead of me, though it's taken me a long time to feel that excitement about my future. I'm not only excited for my future, I'm excited for yours too. Part of what this journey has become for me is the privilege of helping other people to find their way.

My hope is that you've learned something from this book. I know that I learned something about myself in writing it, and I can see my life from a larger vantage point than I did before. It's so easy to see yourself compartmentalized, chopped up into unrelated parts and pieces, but that's not real. Life is one unified string of events that we all experience. What you've just read is my journey to integrating my history into my present. Integration is difficult but essential.

I recognize how unique my childhood was. Your life may or may not have started off in a way that was as strange and unusual as the first twenty years of mine. I do know that people reading this have been through tougher things and have overcome far more than I have.

Whether you started off with a childhood that was easy or tough, simple or complicated, controlled or unregulated, we all must reconcile the past in our present lives today. It's not a simple process for anyone to recode, it takes a lot of hard work.

Don't sit back and live with the weight of your past the way that I did for so long. You deserve better.

If you'd like more resources to help you on your path to unlocking your own Chi Code, I encourage you to visit <u>TheChiCodes.com</u>, where you'll find more information and guidance. I'm here to help. I've been fortunate enough to have help on my way and I truly enjoy mentoring others on their journeys. Reading this one book is not going to change your life, but it can be a catalyst for real and lasting change in your life.

Thank you for reading, and best of luck to you on your path through lifoose one childhood or formative experience and look at it from a different angle with the goal to see it as a positive thing in your life.

CPSIA information can be obtained
at www.ICGtesting.com
Printed in the USA
LVHW111300200420
654125LV00009B/99